Library of Congress Cataloging-in-Publication Data is available.

ISBN 978-1-5235-0425-1

Author: Jennifer Swanson   Reviewer: Kristen Drury
Illustrator: Chris Pearce
Designer: Vanessa Han
Concept by Raquel Jaramillo

Workman books are available at special discounts when purchased in bulk for premiums and sales promotions, as well as for fund-raising or educational use. Special editions or book excerpts can also be created to specification. For details, contact the Special Sales Director at the address below or send an email to specialmarkets@workman.com.

Workman Publishing Co., Inc.
225 Varick Street
New York, NY 10014-4381
workman.com

WORKMAN, BRAIN QUEST, and BIG FAT NOTE-BOOK are registered trademarks of Workman Publishing Co., Inc.

Printed in Thailand

First printing September 2020

10 9 8 7 6 5 4 3 2 1

CHEMISTR

THE **COMPLETE** HIGH SCHOOL STUDY GUIDE

EVERYTHING YOU NEED TO ACE

CHEMISTRY

IN ONE BIG FAT NOTEBOOK

WORKMAN PUBLISHING
NEW YORK

EVERYTHING YOU NEED TO ACE
CHEMISTRY

  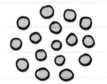 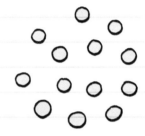

Hi! Welcome to Chemistry !

This notebook is designed to support you as you work through chemistry. Consider this book to be a compilation of notes taken by the smartest person in your chemistry class—the one who seems to "get" everything and takes clear, understandable, accurate notes.

In each chapter, you'll find the important chemistry concepts presented in an easy-to-understand, organized way. Explanations about states and phases of matter, atomic structure and theory, the periodic table, chemical reactions, and more are all presented in a way that makes sense. You don't have to be super smart or a chemistry lover to understand and enjoy the concepts in this book. Think of this book as chemistry for the rest of us.

To help keep things organized:

- Important vocabulary words are highlighted in **YELLOW** and clearly defined.
- Related terms and concepts are written in BLUE INK.
- Examples and calculations are clearly stepped out.
- Concepts are supported by explanations, illustrations, and charts.

If you're not loving your textbook, and you're not so great at taking notes, this notebook will help. It addresses all of the key concepts taught in chemistry class.

CONTENTS

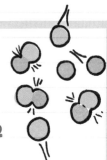

Unit

1

Basics of
Chemistry

Chapter 1

INTRODUCTION TO CHEMISTRY

WHAT IS CHEMISTRY?

Chemistry is the branch of science that studies **MATTER** — what it is and how it changes.

> **MATTER**
> Anything that occupies space and has mass.

Everything you see, touch, hear, smell, and taste involves chemistry and chemicals, which are all matter. Chemistry investigates the properties of matter, how they interact, and how they change.

Chemistry is like cooking. For example, when you're making a hamburger or doing any kind of cooking, you are mixing ingredients— the meat (matter), mashing (applying a force), and grilling (changing the temperature) until you get a hamburger (a new substance).

Chemistry is Everywhere.

Cooking: The creation of food; how and why food rots

Cleaning: The creation and use of detergents, disinfectants, and soaps

Medicine: The creation and use of drugs, vitamins, and supplements

Environment: The creation and spreading of pollutants and the creation of materials to clean up and prevent pollution

TYPES OF CHEMISTRY

Chemistry has different **DISCIPLINES**, or branches. The five main branches are:

ORGANIC CHEMISTRY: The study of carbon-containing compounds in both living and nonliving things.

a chemical substance that has carbon atoms

Methane gas

INORGANIC CHEMISTRY: The study of everything except carbon-based compounds.

BIOCHEMISTRY: The study of the chemical processes that happen inside living things.

PHYSICAL CHEMISTRY: The study of chemical systems as they apply to physics concepts.

LASER BEAM

NUCLEAR CHEMISTRY: The study of chemical changes in the nucleus (center) of an atom. the smallest unit of matter

SCIENTIFIC INQUIRY

Scientists find evidence by conducting experiments and making observations.

The process of using evidence from observation and experiments to create an explanation is called **SCIENTIFIC INQUIRY**. Scientists use a step-by-step method to answer a question. This is called the **SCIENTIFIC METHOD**. It provides scientists with a systematic way to check their work and the work of others.

Scientific inquiry begins with a question or a problem. The scientist tries to collect all of the possible information that relates to the investigation of that question by doing BACKGROUND RESEARCH, making observations, and conducting experiments.

Background research involves reviewing the findings of past scientists to create a HYPOTHESIS, a possible explanation for an observation or problem. Scientists test their hypotheses by making OBSERVATIONS and comparing them to their PREDICTIONS, guesses of what might happen based on previous observations. Observations can require using the senses—the way something looks, smells, feels, or sounds—to describe an event. Observations can be QUANTITATIVE, made in the form of measurements. They can also be QUALITATIVE, describing color, odor, shape, or some OTHER PHYSICAL CHARACTERISTIC. The findings of a scientific inquiry are called RESULTS.

> A **measurement** must have both a number and a unit: for example, 6 inches.

SCIENTIFIC INQUIRY	SCIENTIFIC METHOD
• answers multiple questions • no fixed order of steps	• answers one question • a step-by-step process done in the same order each time • results must be communicated

Scientific Method

Scientists repeat the steps in the scientific method until a hypothesis is proven as either true or false.

The scientific process isn't always straightforward. Scientists often find themselves coming back to the same questions again and again.

Types of Scientific Investigations

Scientists use **PURE SCIENCE** and **APPLIED SCIENCE** to conduct scientific investigations.

PURE SCIENCE

The search for knowledge or facts. It uses theories and predictions to understand nature. Geology is an example of pure science.

APPLIED SCIENCE

Using knowledge in a practical way. Related to engineering and technology. The development of a rocket is an example of applied science.

MAKING A MODEL

A **MODEL** is a representation of a particular situation using something else to represent it. It allows the scientist to easily observe and gather data. There are different kinds of models.

Types of Models

PHYSICAL MODEL:

Something that can be built, such as a molecule that is made of marshmallows, gumdrops, and sticks.

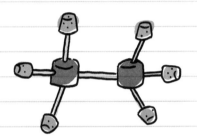

COMPUTER MODEL:

A three-dimensional simulation of a moving object or a chemical reaction.

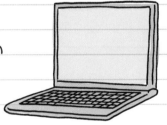

MATHEMATICAL MODEL:

Calculations involving a particular mathematical equation; for example an equation of a line.

$$\frac{dN}{dt} = rN \left(i - \frac{N}{k} \right)$$

SCIENTIFIC THEORIES AND LAWS

After completing many experiments or developing many models, scientists are able to use the results to develop ideas to explain how and why things happen. A scientific idea starts as a hypothesis that has not yet been proven to be true or false.

Once a hypothesis has been proven (through tests and experiments), scientists will develop a **THEORY**.

THEORY

A proposed explanation that is based on an examination of facts. **Facts** can be observed and measured. A theory is a scientist's explanation of the facts.

Theories can be proven or rejected. They can also be changed and improved as more facts are gathered through experimentation or modeling.

Theories are the basis for scientific knowledge. They are a way to take collected facts and put them to practical use.

Theories are the basis for inventions, such as rocket ships to Mars and research, such as finding a cure for cancer.

Scientific laws describe what happens in nature. For example, the French chemist ANTOINE-LAURENT LAVOISIER wrote the LAW OF CONSERVATION OF MASS in 1774. This law states that during a chemical reaction, matter is neither created nor destroyed, just rearranged.

Law of Conservation of Mass

LAW

A rule based on observation of a process in nature
that behaves the same way, each and every time.

A **LAW** describes WHAT happens.

A **THEORY** describes WHY something happens.

CHECK YOUR KNOWLEDGE

1. What is chemistry?

2. How do organic compounds differ from inorganic compounds?

3. Name **three** of the five basic areas of chemistry and what scientists study in these areas.

4. What are two methods for investigating science?

5. Name the basic steps of scientific inquiry.

6. What are models and why are they used in science?

7. What is the difference between a scientific theory and a scientific law?

ANSWERS

13

CHECK YOUR ANSWERS

1. Chemistry is the branch of science that studies matter, what it is, and how it changes.

2. Organic compounds contain carbon and hydrogen bonds. Most inorganic compounds do not contain carbon.

3. Organic chemistry is the study of carbon-containing compounds. Inorganic chemistry is the study of everything except carbon-based compounds. Biochemistry is the chemistry of living things. Physical chemistry is the study of chemical systems in terms of the principles of physics that are used to measure physical properties of substances. Nuclear chemistry is the study of radioactivity and the decay of atoms.

4. Scientists approach their investigations either by searching for pure science (through knowledge and facts) or discovering applied science (using knowledge in a practical way).

5. The basic steps of scientific inquiry are: ask a question, do background research, make a hypothesis, test the hypothesis, analyze results, draw a conclusion, and share the results. If the hypothesis is proven false, another step is to create a new hypothesis.

6. Models are representations of the experiment or object that allows the scientist to easily observe and gather data.

7. A theory is a scientist's explanation of the facts, either measured or observed. A law is a rule based on observation of a process in nature that behaves the same way, every single time.

Chapter 2

CONDUCTING EXPERIMENTS

DESIGNING A SCIENTIFIC EXPERIMENT

Before conducting an experiment, you must plan out exactly what is needed and how you are going to carry out the experiment. Starting points for designing an experiment are:

1. **OBSERVE** something about which you are curious.

2. **CONSTRUCT** a hypothesis.

3. **PLAN** out the experiment to test the hypothesis.

4. **PREDICT** the outcome.

5. CONDUCT the experiment.

6. RECORD the results.

7. REPEAT past experiments to see if you get the same results.

An experiment requires a **PROCEDURE** and a list of materials and methods needed to conduct the experiment.

> **PROCEDURE**
> A step-by-step list of how to carry out the experiment.

You can have a CONTROLLED EXPERIMENT by running the experiment more than once: first without changing any factors (this experiment is called the **CONTROL**) and then a second time, changing only the factor you want to observe. In a controlled experiment, the factors that are not changed are called **CONSTANTS**, and they don't affect the outcome of the experiment.

> **CONTROL**
> A trial during which all of the variables are unchanged. A control is used as the standard comparison for an experiment.

A **VARIABLE** is a factor that can alter your experiment's results—a controlled experiment allows you to test the influence of the variable.

To test only one factor, all other factors in the experiment are held constant, unchanged. This ensures that the changes you observe are caused by the one variable that you changed.

Different variables have different roles.

An INDEPENDENT variable is the variable that you change in an experiment.

A DEPENDENT variable is the variable that is influenced by the independent variable, the results of your experiment.

Every couple of weeks, a teacher has to buy a new goldfish after the previous one has died. The class comes up with a hypothesis that the teacher's goldfish is not getting the right amount of food. They devise an

CONSTANTS:
1. Type of fish
2. Tank size
3. Water quality
4. Water temperature
5. Food type
6. Location

experiment for the teacher to test this factor alone, holding all other variables (type of fish tank, size of fish tank, water quality, water temperature, food type, and location) constant.

In this experiment, the independent variable is the frequency with which the goldfish are fed. The dependent variable is the health of the fish after two weeks.

FEED DAILY

FEED EVERY OTHER DAY

FISH FOOD

EXPERIMENT

CONTROL

COLLECTING DATA

Good data is specific and detailed. They consist of both quantitative and qualitative observations. Measurements must be as **ACCURATE** and **PRECISE** as possible. Make sure that you measure things carefully. Have a notebook ready to record everything as you see it. Keep your notes neat so that they are easy to review. Unreliable (or unreadable) data are useless.

ACCURATE
How close your measured value is to a standard or known value.

PRECISE
How close two or more measured values are to one another.

Bad Measurements

- not accurate but precise
- accurate but not precise
- not accurate and not precise

Measurements should be both accurate and precise.

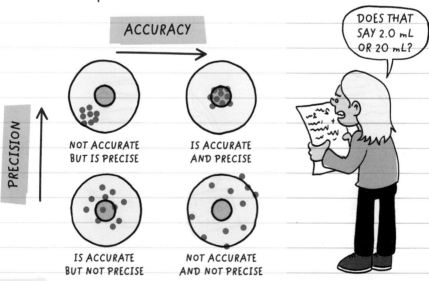

ACCURACY

PRECISION

NOT ACCURATE
BUT IS PRECISE

IS ACCURATE
AND PRECISE

IS ACCURATE
BUT NOT PRECISE

NOT ACCURATE
AND NOT PRECISE

DOES THAT
SAY 2.0 mL
OR 20 mL?

PRESENTING DATA

After collecting data, you can present it in many different, more quantitative ways. For example:

TABLES present data in rows and columns. Because all of the numbers are close to each other, these are easy to read and compare. A table is a fast and easy way to record data during an experiment.

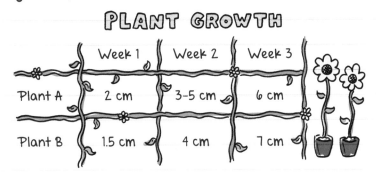

PLANT GROWTH

	Week 1	Week 2	Week 3
Plant A	2 cm	3-5 cm	6 cm
Plant B	1.5 cm	4 cm	7 cm

BAR GRAPHS present data as bars of varying heights or lengths. This is an easy way to compare different variables. The taller, or longer, the bar, the larger the number.

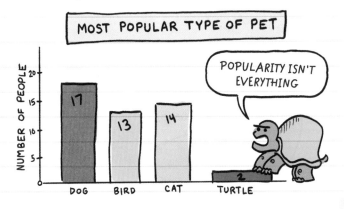

MOST POPULAR TYPE OF PET

NUMBER OF PEOPLE

DOG 17 BIRD 13 CAT 14 TURTLE 2

POPULARITY ISN'T EVERYTHING

LINE GRAPHS show the relationship between two variables. The independent variable is plotted on the x-axis (the horizontal line), and the dependent variable is on the y-axis (the vertical line). Each axis has a scale to show the intervals of the measurements. Scales are done in even increments, such as 1, 2, 3, 4 or 2, 4, 6, 8. Line graphs show continuous change over time. . . .

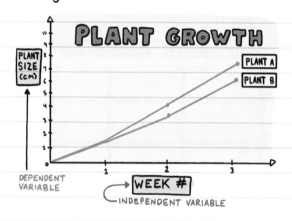

CIRCLE GRAPHS: Think of this as a "pie" chart. Each piece of data is represented by a "slice" of the pie.

FAVORITE HOT DOG TOPPINGS

8 CHOSE MUSTARD
6 CHOSE KETCHUP
4 CHOSE KETCHUP
+ MUSTARD
2 CHOSE ONIONS

KETCHUP + MUSTARD

MUSTARD

ONIONS

KETCHUP

ANALYZING DATA

Analyzing data is comparing and examining the information collected. This is something that all scientists need to do to determine the outcome of their experiment. Data is usually shown in the form of a diagram or graph. You compare the variables that are being tested against the ones that are being kept the same. It is important to compare your data accurately so that you can determine exactly what happened during your experiment. That way you will be able to repeat the experiment if needed.

Which type of graph is best to show the data?

LINE GRAPH If your data has small changes in it, for example, an increase from .01 to .06, you can use a line graph. This format makes small differences more visible.

CIRCLE GRAPH If you want to show changes as part of a whole, use a circle graph. For example, if you need to record how much of an hour was spent on various tasks, this format would be good to use.

BAR GRAPH If you are tracking large changes over a period of time, or groups of numbers, a bar graph might be best. For example, if you have different cars and you want to compare their top speeds against each other.

DRAWING CONCLUSIONS

You have reached the end of your experiment. Did the results support your hypothesis? Why or why not? Even if your results did not support your hypothesis, you can still learn from them. It is important to explain in your conclusion why you think your hypothesis was wrong. Were there sources of experimental error, or did the procedure need to be changed?

Sometimes, the conclusions aren't immediately obvious and you will have to **INFER**, or use observations and facts to reach a conclusion about something you may not have directly witnessed.

For example, if you want to find out what a Tyrannosaurus rex ate, you might observe the types of fossilized droppings that could be found near its fossils. If you see crushed bones, you might infer that the dinosaur ate smaller animals or other dinosaurs.

> When you need to infer, it can help to look at background information and do further research.

CHECK YOUR KNOWLEDGE

1. What are the two ways that data can be measured?

2. What graphs can be used to present data?

3. If the results from your experiment don't support your hypothesis, was the experiment a failure or a success? Explain your answer.

4. What is the difference between being accurate and being precise?

5. Why is it important to correctly analyze your data from an experiment?

6. You have collected data that shows large changes during a period of time. What type of graph would you use for this?

7. When would you use a line graph?

ANSWERS

CHECK YOUR ANSWERS

1. Data is either quantitative, in the form of specific measurements, or qualitative and based on the way something looks, feels, smells, or sounds.

2. Three different graphs that are used to present data are line, bar, and circle graphs.

3. If the results from your experiment don't support your hypothesis, it does not necessarily mean that your experiment was a failure. Scientists can learn from every experiment. If the data doesn't support the hypothesis, then you can ask why and try to figure out any factors that may have affected the experiment.

4. Accuracy is determined using the closeness of the value that is measured to a standard or known value. Precision is determined through the closeness of two or more measured values to each other.

5. You need to correctly analyze your data so that you can compare your results to multiple experiments if needed.

6. A bar graph would be best for this data.

7. If your data shows small changes over time.

Chapter 3

LAB REPORTS AND EVALUATING RESULTS

It's important for scientists to share their results with others in their field. That way, they can learn from them, critique them, and even build on them.

Atoms, the basic building blocks of matter, were first discovered by the Greek philosopher DEMOCRITUS. Democritus was also the first to call them "atoms." JOHN DALTON adopted Democritus's ideas and used them to form the FIRST MODERN ATOMIC MODEL. Dalton shared his results about atoms and how atoms were

formed. This allowed the knowledge of the structure of the atom to grow and expand over the years through the discoveries of different scientists.

There are many ways to communicate your findings. You can give a speech, write an article for a scientific journal, or give an interview. The first step to communicating your findings is to write a LAB REPORT.

WRITING A LAB REPORT

A lab report is made up of different parts:

TITLE: Tells the reader about the experiment or investigation.

INTRODUCTION/PURPOSE: Gives a brief description of the question that is being asked or why the investigation is being done. "What question am I trying to answer?" "What is the purpose of this study?" It can also include any research that may already exist about the topic.

HYPOTHESIS-PREDICTION: States specifically what you think will happen in the investigation and why.

MATERIALS AND EQUIPMENT: Lists all of the materials and equipment that are necessary to carry out the investigation. You can even add a diagram or sketch of the materials needed for the setup.

PROCEDURE: Describes the entire step-by-step process that is followed during the investigation. Imagine yourself instructing someone who is completely unfamiliar with the experiment. The process should be as clear as possible.

DATA/RESULTS: Gives a concise account of all of the measurements and observations that you made during the investigation. This should be presented in an organized manner. It is helpful to use graphs, tables, charts, drawings, or even photographs. The most important part of the data is accuracy and precision.

An accurate player hits the center every time. A precise player hits the same spot every time.

> **CONCLUSION/EVALUATION:** Presents a summary of what you learned from the investigation. This can include a claim, evidence, and reasoning, in which you answer the initial question with a claim and show how your evidence supports the claim.

EVALUATING RESULTS

When you read another scientist's lab report, think critically about the findings and ask yourself questions:

- Was the procedure followed exactly?
- What sources of error may have affected the experimental results?
- When were the observations made—during the experiment or afterward?
- Is the given conclusion supported by the data that were collected?
- Was the hypothesis supported?
- Is there another way to interpret the data?
- Can the results be replicated or reproduced?

Results are not always (conclusive) (leading to a definite answer). Sometimes they are (inconclusive.)

The opposite of this.

That does not mean that the investigation was a waste (or that you got it wrong). Maybe the answers that you were looking for cannot be found by using this specific investigation.

How do you find the answers that you are looking for?

- Change the variables.
- Design a new model.
- Try a different investigation.

Sources of Experimental Error

There can be sources of error in any type of measurement. This means that if you measure a quantity once and then a second time, you may get a different reading. This is normal, but you should always try to be consistent when you measure. Sometimes getting the exact same outcome twice is not possible.

Every investigation has two types of errors: **SYSTEMATIC** and **RANDOM**.

SYSTEMATIC ERRORS

A systemic error affects the accuracy of a measurement. If the instrument that you are using is not properly set, it cannot give an accurate measurement. **CALIBRATION** is when the readings of an instrument are compared to a known measurement to check its accuracy. This can also be known as "zeroing" something. For example, if you turn on a digital scale, does it read zero without anything on it? Or does it read .01 grams (g) or .02 g? If the reading is not zero, then the scale is not properly calibrated. This will affect all of the measurements that you take on this scale.

Perhaps the scale isn't digital but is read with a lever that moves into position. Are you looking at the lever straight on or at an angle? If you read the lever at a different angle each time, you will get a different measurement each time.

A **parallax error** occurs when you view the object from different points. The correct answer is indicated by the straight green arrow and number.

19.82 mL
19.70 mL
19.62 mL
20

RANDOM ERRORS

A random error is caused by errors in the experimental apparatus or by the person who is reading the measurement. Random errors affect the precision of the measurement.

For example, if you step on a scale, it may say that you weigh 150.2 lbs, then 150.1 lbs, and then 149.8 lbs. The numbers jump around. Why is there a difference? The scale is simply fluctuating back and forth. Sometimes that occurs because you have made a tiny movement or the scale itself is not sensitive enough to register a more accurate reading.

Reporting Experimental Error

It's difficult to get an accurate and precise measurement. In every lab report, scientists need to report the accuracy and precision of the measurements as well as possible sources of experimental error. This is so that other scientists reading the report understand the limitations of the results.

ANEMOMETER

- For example, did the results come from a scale that was not calibrated to zero?

- Was the investigation conducted on a windy day, which may have interfered with the reading of the lever on the scale?

- Might moisture have affected the mass reading of a sample that was assumed to be dry?

- Did the coarseness of the filter paper used in a funnel allow fine particles to pass through unaccounted for?

Just because it is impossible to be completely accurate and precise doesn't mean that you shouldn't make your best effort to be as accurate and precise as possible.

Significant Figures

Sometimes it is impossible to get an exact measurement, especially if you don't have sensitive tools. Perhaps your equipment only produces measurements in whole numbers and, for example, can't go to one-tenth (0.1) or one-hundredth (0.01). The precision of a measurement is determined by the number of digits reported. The more precise the measurement tool, the more precise and accurate the measurements will be. For example, 2.75 cm is a more accurate reading than 2.7 cm.

The numbers reported in a measurement are called **SIGNIFICANT FIGURES**. These are all of the known figures plus one estimated digit. This estimated digit is called the **SIGNIFICANT DIGIT**, and scientists reach it by using estimation or by rounding numbers.

A **SIGNIFICANT DIGIT** is the number that provides the most exact measurement possible. For example, in this thermometer, it appears that the lines are set to be 2 degrees apart. The arrow between the two lines indicates that the temperature can be read to be between 138 and 140 degrees. Because you can't be sure of the exact temperature, you will need to estimate the answer to 139 degrees.

ESTIMATION: A rough guess of the measurement using observation and reasoning.

ROUNDING: Picking the closest number to the specified place value based on the accuracy of the equipment. For example, if you are rounding to the tens place and the number is 5 or higher, you round up. If the number is 4 or lower, you round down.

CALCULATING PERCENT ERROR

PERCENT ERROR is the difference between a measured value and a known value expressed as a percentage. Percent error shows how far the experimental value is from the accepted value, when compared with the size of the actual value. This is important because <u>percent error tells you about your measurement's accuracy</u>.

To calculate percent error, subtract the accepted value (A) from the experimental value (E) (or vice versa, because you will report the absolute value of this difference). Divide that difference by A, the accepted value. Then multiply by 100.

$$\text{Percent error} = \frac{|E - A|}{|A|} \times 100$$

Accepted value is known to be true and can be found in a standard reference.

Experimental value is the value that you actually measured.

The percent error can be small or large. For example, if the accepted value of the data is 35.67 g and the measured value is 35.62 g, the percent error is 0.14%. However, if the accepted value is 5 g and the measured value is 0.5 g, percent error is 90%, which is much larger.

CHECK YOUR KNOWLEDGE

1. Explain why it's important to share the results of your investigation with other scientists.

2. Must a hypothesis always be proven correct for an investigation to be successful? Explain your answer.

3. Explain the difference between precision and accuracy.

4. What does it mean to calibrate an instrument?

5. What should you include in a conclusion?

6. Describe a situation where you might need to use estimation or round numbers.

7. Why is it important to include percent error in your report?

ANSWERS

CHECK YOUR ANSWERS

1. As a scientist, it's important to share your results with others in your field. That way they can learn from them, critique them, and even build on them.

2. No. (A prediction is an idea of what might happen.) Disproving a hypothesis does not make the experiment wrong. It can simply mean that you believed one idea but observed conflicting results.

3. Accuracy is how close your measurement is to a standard or known value. Precision is how consistent your measurements are to one another.

4. Calibration occurs when the readings of an instrument are correlated with a standard to check its accuracy. This can also be known as "zero-ing."

5. In your conclusion, include a summary of what you learned from the investigation, whether your results supported your hypothesis, any sources of experimental error, and any questions that you might have for future investigations. A conclusion can also include your interpretation of the results and how they relate to existing scientific theory and knowledge.

6. Sometimes it is impossible to get an exact measurement, especially if you don't have the right tools. Perhaps your equipment only measures in whole numbers and can't read to one-tenth (0.1) or one-hundredth (0.01) of a number. In these cases when a guess is necessary, scientists use estimation or rounding numbers.

7. In every lab report, scientists need to report the accuracy and precision of the measurements via percent error. This is done so that other scientists reading the report understand the limitations of the results.

Chapter 4

MEASUREMENT

The International System of Units, or **SI SYSTEM**, is the preferred method of measurement in chemistry. It has a base unit for every type of measurement.

> **SI**
> An abbreviation for the French term SYSTÈME INTERNATIONALE, which translates to "International System."

TYPE OF MEASURE	SI BASE UNIT
length (or distance)	meter (m)
mass	gram (g)
weight (or force)	newton (N)
volume (or capacity)	liter (L)
temperature	Kelvin (K)
time	second (s)
pressure	Newtons per square meter (N/m^2) (Pascal)
electric current	ampere (A)
amount of substrate	mole (mol)

Scientists devised a system of prefixes that multiplies the base unit by factors of 10. By switching the prefix, an SI unit can be used for large and small measurements.

SI PREFIX	MULTIPLIER	POWER OF TEN
giga (G)	1,000,000,000	10^9
mega (M)	1,000,000	10^6
kilo (k)	1,000	10^3
hecto (h)	100	10^2
deca (da)	10	10^1
(base unit)	1	10^0
deci (d)	0.1	10^{-1}
centi (c)	0.01	10^{-2}
milli (m)	0.001	10^{-3}
micro (μ)	0.000001	10^{-6}
nano (n)	0.000000001	10^{-9}

Mnemonic for SI Prefixes:

Great Mighty King Henry Died By Drinking Chunky Milk Monday Night.

DIMENSIONAL ANALYSIS

DIMENSIONAL ANALYSIS is a mathematical method used to convert actual measured units into the units needed for the answer to a problem.

A **CONVERSION FACTOR** is the relationship between the two units.

A conversion factor is also known as a **RATIO.**

Suppose a model car measures 15 cm long. How many inches is that?

First you need to know the conversion factor from inches (in.) to centimeters (cm).

The conversion factor for inches to centimeters is 1 in. = 2.54 cm.

The conversion factor can be written three ways:

1 in. = 2.54 cm

OR $\dfrac{1 \text{ in.}}{2.54 \text{ cm}}$

OR $\dfrac{2.54 \text{ cm}}{1 \text{ in.}}$

The factor that you use depends on the units that you originally have and the units that you need to find.

In this case, you need to know how many inches, so you would use this factor: $\dfrac{1 \text{ in.}}{2.54 \text{ cm}}$

This is so the unit in the numerator (inches) can cancel the same units in the denominator (centimeters).

Multiply the given length (15 cm) by the number of inches in the conversion and divide by the number of centimeters. The answer will be in inches:

$$15 \text{ cm} \times \dfrac{1 \text{ in.}}{2.54 \text{ cm}} = \dfrac{15}{2.54} = 5.9055 \text{ in.}$$

So, the length of the model car is 5.9055 inches.

Dimensional analysis is a method for solving problems that involves canceling out the same units to multiply by a factor of 1.

If you have something measured in kilometers and need to read it in centimeters, dimensional analysis would involve this process:

1. Convert to meters.

$$1 \text{ km} \times \frac{1,000 \text{ m}}{1 \text{ km}} = 1,000 \text{ m}$$

2. Then convert from meters to centimeters.

$$1,000 \text{ m} \times \frac{100 \text{ cm}}{1 \text{ m}} = 100,000 \text{ cm}$$

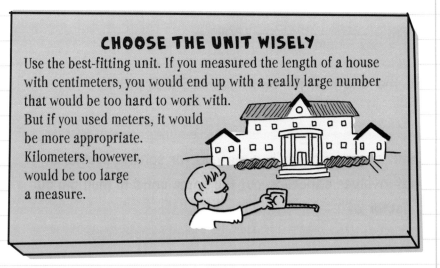

CHOOSE THE UNIT WISELY

Use the best-fitting unit. If you measured the length of a house with centimeters, you would end up with a really large number that would be too hard to work with. But if you used meters, it would be more appropriate. Kilometers, however, would be too large a measure.

TYPES OF MEASUREMENT

The SI system has a standard unit for every type of measure.

LENGTH → METER (m): Distance between two points.

VOLUME → LITER (L): Amount of space that something occupies.

MASS → GRAM (g): Amount of matter in a solid, liquid, or gas.

WEIGHT → NEWTON (N): Force exerted by a mass by a gravitational field. ←

When you measure someone's weight, you measure the force that they exert on the earth.

Mass and weight are NOT the same.

> Weight relies on gravity (a force).
> Mass is the amount of matter in an object.
>
> ## Weight = (mass) × (gravity)
> ### OR
> ## W = mg

If you go to the moon, you will still have the same mass, but you will be weightless. That is because the moon's gravity is $\frac{1}{6}$ that of the Earth's.

TIME → SECONDS (s): Period between events. The SI unit is seconds, but you can also use minutes, hours, days, months, and years.

DENSITY → GRAMS (per liter or Kg/m³, which is the same as g/L): amount of mass per unit volume. In chemistry, units of density are often recorded as g/mL (grams per milliliter) or g/cm³ (grams per centimeter cubed).

TEMPERATURE → KELVIN (K): Measure of the average kinetic energy of the atoms or molecules in a system.

> Temperature and heat are NOT the same.

HEAT → CALORIE (cal): Total energy of the molecular motion in a substance.

The SI units for temperature is Kelvin (K), but most scientists instead use Celsius (C), another SI-derived unit.

The formula to convert *Celsius* to *Kelvin* is

Temperature in Celsius

$$T_K = T_{°C} + 273.15$$

OR

$$T_{°C} = T_K - 273.15$$

Temperature in Kelvin

Kelvin does not use a degree symbol.

In the U.S., Fahrenheit is used to measure temperature.
This is the formula to convert Fahrenheit to Celsius:

Temperature in Fahrenheit

$$T_{°F} = (T_{°C} \times \frac{9}{5}) + 32$$

OR

Temperature in Celsius

$$T_{°C} = (T_{°F} - 32) \times \frac{5}{9}$$

Another way of saying this is:

$$°F = 1.8°C + 32 \quad \text{and} \quad °C = \frac{(°F - 32)}{1.8}$$

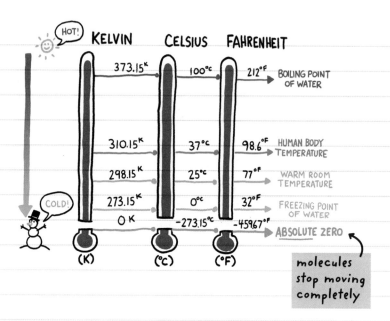

PRESSURE: Measure of the force exerted on a unit area of surface.

The SI unit for pressure is **Newtons per square meter (N/m²)**—also called Pascals. The more commonly used units in chemistry are either **Pascals (Pa)** or **atmospheres (atm)**.

(kPa stands for kiloPascal. 1,000 Pa = 1 kPa.)

$$1 \text{ Pa} = 1 \text{ N/m}^2$$

$$1 \text{ atm} = 101.325 \text{ kPa} = 101,325 \text{ Pa}$$

Standard atmospheric pressure, the actual pressure at sea level, is defined as:

$$1 \text{ atm}, 1.013 \times 10^5 \text{ Pa, or } 101.3 \text{ kPa}$$

USING SIGNIFICANT FIGURES

Significant figures are important for accuracy and precision. The digits reported must be to the place actually measured, with one estimated digit, based on the accuracy of the equipment itself. This allows measurements to be compared correctly. For example, if a graduated cylinder has visible lines that show the tens, ones, and tenths places, the final measurement is reported to the hundredths place. This is the last "actual" measurement line that we can see (tenths), plus an estimation of one place beyond (hundredths).

Measurements must be in exact significant figures, which are determined by the precision of the measuring tool; in this case, a ruler. The pencil can correctly be measured to the tenths position in both inches and centimeters.

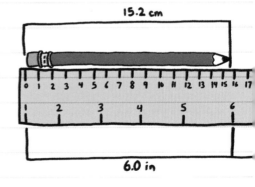

15.2 cm

6.0 in

Rules for Significant Figures

1. All nonzero digits are significant; they always count.

For example, a recording of 452 mL has three signifcant figures (sig figs).

2. Zero values that are "sandwiched" between nonzero digits are significant; they always count. It doesn't matter whether there is a decimal in the measurement or not.

For example:
23.608 g has five sig figs.
608 g has three sig figs.
8.04 g has three sig figs.

3. Zero values that are not "sandwiched" between nonzero digits:

• If a decimal point is present, read the value from left to right. Start counting significant figures beginning with the first nonzero digit. Count the zeros at the end of the number.

For example:

0.35 g (two sig figs)

0.098 g (two sig figs)

0.0980 g (three sig figs)

0.09800 g (four sig figs)

0.098000 g (five sig figs) ← This number of significant figures means greater accuracy—and usually more expensive equipment used.

6.0 g (two sig figs)

6.00 g (three sig figs)

If a decimal point is NOT present, read the value from right to left: Start counting significant figures with the first nonzero digit.

For example:

Start counting with this number.

580 g (two sig figs)

Don't count this.

5800 g (two sig figs)

6060 mm (three sig figs)

500 mg (one sig fig)

DIFFERENT ACCURACIES

What happens when two measurement devices have different accuracies? For example, a balance measures mass to two significant figures and a graduated cylinder measures volume to four significant figures. How many significant figures can you include in your recorded measurement and still maintain accuracy?

The total number of significant figures in the final reported value can be no more than the significant figures in the least accurate measurement. In other words, the calculated answer can be no more accurate than the measurement made by the least accurate piece of lab equipment.

FOR EXAMPLE:

The least number of sig figs is two, so this is the least accurate measurement.

If an object has mass of 32 g and a volume of 18.01 mL, its density (mass divided by volume) is given as having two significant figures.

CHECK YOUR KNOWLEDGE

1. What is the difference between mass and weight?

2. What are the two different units that can be used to express pressure?

3. What is the formula to convert Celsius to Fahrenheit? Convert 65 degrees Celsius to degrees Fahrenheit.

4. What is a conversion factor and how it is used? Give the conversion factor for inches to centimeters.

5. Convert 3.45 feet to centimeters.

6. What is the difference between heat and temperature?

7. Why do you need to use significant figures?

8. When rounding, how do you know when to round up or down?

ANSWERS

CHECK YOUR ANSWERS

1. Mass is the amount of matter in a solid, liquid, or gas. Weight is the force exerted by a mass in a gravitational field.

2. Two different units that are used to express pressure are atmospheres and Pascals (Newtons per meters squared).

3. The calculation to convert Celsius to Fahrenheit is $T_{°F} = (T_{°C} \times \frac{9}{5}) + 32$. The calculation to convert 65 degrees Celsius to degrees Fahrenheit is $T_{°F} = (65 \times \frac{9}{5}) + 32$ $T_{°F} = 149°$.

4. A conversion factor is the relationship between two units.

   Conversion factors can be written one of three ways:

   1 in. = 2.54 cm OR $\frac{1 \text{ in.}}{2.54 \text{ cm}}$ OR $\frac{2.54 \text{ cm}}{1 \text{ in.}}$

5. The conversion factor is 5,280 ft = 1.609 km and 1 km = 100,000 cm,

   so $3.45 \text{ ft} \times \frac{1.609 \text{ km}}{5,280 \text{ ft}} \times \frac{100,000 \text{ cm}}{1 \text{ km}} = 105 \text{ cm}$.

6. Heat is total energy of the molecular motion in a substance. Temperature is a measure of the average kinetic energy of atoms or molecules in a system.

7. Significant figures are important for accuracy and precision. The digits reported must be to the place actually measured, not guessed. This allows measurements to be compared correctly.

8. When rounding, if the number at the end is 5 or greater, the number is rounded up. If the number at the end is 4 or less, the number is rounded down.

Chapter 5

LAB SAFETY AND SCIENTIFIC TOOLS

LAB SAFETY

The most important rule to remember in a chemistry lab is **SAFETY FIRST!**

USE COMMON SENSE. IT COULD SAVE YOUR LIFE.

- Be cautious.

- Always pay attention.

- Follow both written and verbal directions.

GENERAL LAB SAFETY RULES

The following rules must be strictly followed in any laboratory setting.

Do not enter the lab without your teacher or another qualified adult present.

Wear safety goggles at all times, even during cleanup. Prescription glasses are okay when worn under safety goggles.

Wear your lab coat or apron and gloves when instructed. This is to keep you safe from chemical spills or burns.

Dress appropriately. No sandals or open-toed shoes, loose clothing, or dangling or excessive jewelry. Make sure long hair is tied back; otherwise, it could catch on fire easily.

Don't eat, drink, or chew gum in the lab. Be sure to wash your hands before you leave the lab. You don't want to accidentally eat anything left over from your experiment.

Keep your lab area clean and organized by putting your coat and backpack under your seat or in a specially designated place.

If you or someone else is injured, notify the teacher **immediately**.

NO RUNNING OR THROWING THINGS IN THE LAB. KEEP EVERYONE SAFE!

Leave your lab area the way you found it, with clean instruments and glassware.

Waste Disposal

Every experiment will generate some sort of waste. There could be leftover mixtures, solids that you produced, or even just bits of paper from a litmus test. Everything has a place where it can be properly discarded.

Follow these directions to discard waste:

1. Only authorized household chemicals and solutions and water can go down the sink. Otherwise, if it has any type of chemical in it, don't allow it to go down the drain.

2. Use the proper waste container for the type of waste that you have:

- Solid waste must be discarded to a solid waste container.

- Broken glass must be placed into a broken glass collector. Never discard broken glass with regular trash.

- Chemical waste that is in the form of a liquid or solution must go into the appropriately labeled waste bottle or be neutralized when appropriate.

(DO NOT mix waste.)

3. Only place regular trash into garbage cans.

When Working with Chemicals

- Read every label <u>twice</u> to make sure that you have the proper chemical.

- DO <u>NOT</u> conduct unauthorized experiments.

chemicals used

- Do not take reagent bottles away from their places. Carry liquids to your bench in clean test tubes or beakers, and carry solids in clean glassware or on weighing paper.

- Take only the amount of reagent indicated. Larger amounts will not be more effective and may lead to uncontrollable reactions. (Plus, it's wasteful, and many chemicals are expensive.)

- Never return unused chemicals to stock bottles. Dispose of them properly, according to instructions.

- Never use the same pipette for different chemicals. Do not insert your pipette or dropper into the reagent bottles. Use the one that is labeled for that reagent.

- If an acid is to be diluted, pour acid slowly into the water with constant stirring to minimize spattering and disperse heat. Never add water directly to acid.

SAFETY EQUIPMENT

Each chemistry lab is equipped with many different pieces of safety equipment. Know how to use the equipment and where it is located.

If an accident happens, TELL THE TEACHER!

EYE WASH: Use if a chemical spills or splashes into your eye. Immediately rinse your eye for a minimum of 15 minutes straight.

THERMAL TONGS OR MITTS: Use these to handle hot equipment such as beakers and flasks. Hot glass looks the same as cool glass.

FIRE EXTINGUISHER: Use to put out electrical, chemical, or gas fires. To use, remember the acronym PASS (Pull, Aim, Squeeze, Sweep).

FIRE BLANKET: Use to smother a fire on a person or small surfaces. If a person is on fire, wrap them in the blanket and have them "STOP, DROP, and ROLL."

SAFETY SHOWER : Use only if a chemical is spilled directly on clothes or skin. Before entering, remove all contaminated clothing. Once in the shower, rinse yourself for a minimum of 15 minutes.

Final Tips

When you are working with:

HEAT

Never leave a heat source unattended.

CRACK!

Never heat something in a closed container.

CHEMICALS

Don't ever taste them or smell them directly.

THE BEST WAY TO SMELL A CHEMICAL IS BY WAFTING IT TOWARD YOUR NOSE WITH YOUR HAND.

Never use chemicals from an unlabeled container.

ELECTRICITY

Ensure that cords are not frayed or damaged and keep them neat so that no one trips on them.

Do NOT allow water to get near electrical outlets or equipment.

LAB TOOLS AND INSTRUMENTS

A **BEAKER** looks like a glass cup with a spout at the top rim to make pouring liquids easy. Lines on the sides indicate rough measurements, most likely milliliters, but these are not exact and should only be used when estimating volume or when approximate amounts are needed.

An **ERLENMEYER FLASK** looks like a beaker, but it's narrower at the top. This makes it easier to place a stopper in it so that you can save the contents for later. The measurements on this flask would also be approximated to the nearest milliliter.

VOLUMETRIC FLASKS are rounded at the bottom and have a long, skinny neck. They are used for more precise volume measurements than an Erlenmeyer flask, especially when preparing solutions of a specified concentration. They only have one mark for a very specific volume.

STOPPERS are usually rubber tops that fit into flasks or test tubes. Sometimes, they are closed at the top and have small holes that allow them to be fitted to another piece of equipment.

A **TEST TUBE** is a glass tube that's rounded at the end. Think of it as a long, hollow finger.

But don't put a test tube ON your finger. Ouch!

A **TEST TUBE BRUSH** is used to clean out the inside of test tubes.

FUNNELS are cone-shaped objects with stems. They are used to help pour liquids or solutions from one container to another.

Be SURE to use the right funnel for the right container.

FILTER PAPER is a piece of round, flat paper that is used for filtering solids or precipitates to separate them from liquids or solutions. They must be folded properly to fit into the funnel.

Be SURE to fold the filter paper in half first, then again, then peel back one layer before putting into the funnel.

A **GRADUATED CYLINDER** is used to measure liquids or solutions and is fairly accurate to the 0.1 place.

When measuring a liquid or solution, be SURE to read the bottom of the **MENISCUS**, the curved surface of the liquid.

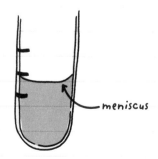

meniscus

A **PIPETTE** is a long, thin tube with a suction attached. This allows you to draw up the correct amount of liquid, check the measurement on the side, and transfer the liquid to another container.

A **BURETTE AND STAND** is a long, thin pipe with a valve and stopcock at the end. The burette is held in place by a ring stand with a burette clamp that holds the burette. The burette has precise calculations so that you can deliver the correct amount of solution for the experiment, usually accurate to the 0.01 place.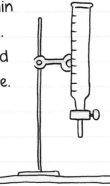

 A **BUNSEN BURNER** is used for heating things. It is actually an open flame that is fed by a gas line. Bunsen burners are hooked to the gas line via rubber tubing. The amount of gas is controlled by turning the valve at the hookup point or by adjusting the Bunsen burner itself.

Do NOT turn the flame up too high!

A **RING STAND** is a circle of metal attached to a stand that can hold beakers or flasks up in the air when supported by a wire gauze or clay triangle. Adjust the height by moving the knob on the side of the stand.

A **HOT PLATE** is for heating things, but unlike the Bunsen burner, it does not have an open flame. A dial controls the temperature of the heating plate.

An **ELECTRONIC BALANCE** is used to measure the mass of a substance. Just put the substance onto the balance (always in a container or on a piece of weighing paper) and read the number on the digital display. Never place chemicals directly onto the pan of an electronic balance.

A **DOUBLE PAN BALANCE** is used to compare the weight of two different objects. To make it work, you must first know the mass of one of the objects. Place the second object in the other pan, and when the two pans are level, the masses are the same.

WEIGHING BOAT OR WEIGHING PAPER is used to hold the substance to be massed.

Make sure to get the mass of the boat FIRST before you add your substance. Then you can subtract and get the actual mass of the substance. If your balance has a "TARE" button, push this to "zero" the balance and automatically subtract the mass of the boat first.

SCOOPULAS AND SPATULAS are small metal or plastic curved tools to help transfer solid substances from one container to another.

pestle

A **MORTAR AND PESTLE** is used to grind larger pieces into powder. The mortar is the round bowl and the pestle is the tool used to grind the solid.

mortar

A **THERMOMETER** is for measuring temperature, usually in Celsius.

CHECK YOUR KNOWLEDGE

1. What is the most important thing to remember in a chemistry lab?

2. What required safety gear must be worn in the lab?

3. What is the best way to smell a chemical?

4. What do you do if you splash a chemical into your eyes?

5. A _____ stand is used to hold a beaker over a Bunsen burner.

6. What do you do with unused or leftover chemicals?

7. What is a pipette? What is one thing you must NEVER do while using it?

8. Describe how you would safely dilute an acid with water.

9. How do you get the correct mass of a substance when using a weighing boat?

ANSWERS

CHECK YOUR ANSWERS

1. Safety first! Always pay attention to what you are doing. Read labels. Double-check everything. No goofing off. Be professional.

2. Goggles and a lab coat are required safety gear. Hair must be tied back, and no open-toed shoes or sandals are permitted in the lab.

3. Waft it toward your nose with your hand. Do NOT stick your nose into or directly over the beaker/flask/bottle.

4. If you spill a chemical into your eyes, have someone notify the teacher while you go to the eye wash and rinse out your eye(s) for a minimum of 15 minutes.

5. A ring stand is used to hold a beaker over a Bunsen burner.

6. Never return unused chemicals to stock bottles. Dispose of properly in the appropriately labeled container.

7. A pipette is a long, thin tube with a suction tube attached. This allows you to draw up the correct amount of liquid (check the measurement on the side) and transfer the liquid to another container. NEVER use your mouth to suck up the liquid into the pipette.

8. If an acid is to be diluted, pour acid slowly into the water, with constant stirring. Never add water to acid. The acid is more dense than water and will sink to the bottom, beneath the water, which will reduce the amount of acid splashing out of the container as it is being poured.

9. Find the mass of the weighing boat empty first, then add the substance. Subtract the mass of the weighing boat from the total to get the mass of the substance.

Unit

2

All About Matter

Chapter 6

PROPERTIES OF MATTER AND CHANGES IN FORM

MATTER is anything that occupies space and has mass. If you can see, touch, taste, smell, or feel it, then it's matter.

PROPERTIES OF MATTER

A **PROPERTY** describes how an object looks, feels, or acts. All properties of matter are classified as either **physical** or **chemical**.

Physical Properties

A **PHYSICAL PROPERTY** can usually be observed with our senses. Physical properties include:

COLOR (quality of an object or substance with respect to the reflection of light)

SIZE (an object's overall dimensions)

VOLUME (the amount of space a substance or object occupies)

DENSITY (ratio of mass and volume in a substance)

BOILING POINT/MELTING POINT (temperature at which something boils or melts)

MAGNETISM (whether or not something is magnetic)

SOLUBILITY (how easily something dissolves in another substance)

EXTENSIVE AND INTENSIVE PROPERTIES

Physical properties are broken down into two different categories: **INTENSIVE** and **EXTENSIVE PROPERTIES**.

Intensive properties do NOT depend on the amount of the substance present; for example, density. The density of a substance (at room remperature) is the same no matter how much of the substance that you have.

Extensive properties depend on the amount of matter being measured. For example, mass, length, and volume measures depend on how much of the object that you have.

For example, you can have 10 mg or 10 kg of substance, but it makes no difference if you are measuring the intensive property of that substance. However, it makes a huge difference if you are measuring the extensive property.

10 mg

10 Kg

INTENSIVE PROPERTIES INCLUDE:

- Color
- Odor
- Temperature
- Freezing point
- Melting point
- Boiling point
- Density
- State of matter
- Malleability
- Ductility

EXTENSIVE PROPERTIES INCLUDE:

- Size
- Length
- Width
- Volume
- Mass
- Weight

Extensive properties can be added together. For example, two pennies will have more mass than one penny. That's because the mass of two is greater than the mass of one.

Chemical Properties

A **CHEMICAL PROPERTY** is any characteristic that can be determined only by changing a substance's identity, possibly through a chemical reaction.

Chemical properties include: **REACTIVITY** with other chemicals, **TOXICITY**, **FLAMMABILITY**, and **COMBUSTIBILITY**.

REACTIVITY: the likelihood of a substance to undergo a chemical reaction

TOXICITY: how poisonous or damaging a chemical substance may be to organisms

FLAMMABILITY: whether a substance will burn when exposed to a flame

COMBUSTIBILITY: the measure of how easily a substance will burn in oxygen

Determining Properties of Matter

↓

Can you identify the properties of this substance without changing it?

No ↙   ↘ Yes

Chemical property   Physical property

PHYSICAL AND CHEMICAL CHANGES

The changes that matter experiences are classified as either **physical** or **chemical**.

A **PHYSICAL CHANGE** is any alteration to the size, shape, or state (solid, liquid, or gas) of a substance. The final changes take place without altering the substance's molecular composition.

The final substance is made of the same matter as before the change.

A **CHEMICAL CHANGE** occurs when matter changes into a new substance and has a new chemical property. Chemical changes **DO** alter the molecular makeup of the substance.

The final substance is NOT made of the same matter as before the change.

Log → log ashes: NOT the same.

How do you know when something has undergone a chemical change?

Look for one of these signs:

CHANGE in **COLOR:** This is similar to what occurs when you leave a sliced apple out of the refrigerator, and it turns brown.

CHANGE in **ODOR:** A smell is given off. It can be an unpleasant smell, like rotten food.

FORMATION of a **GAS:** Mixing two substances that emit a gas, such as vinegar and baking soda, which releases bubbles. Bubbles show that a gas has formed.

FORMATION of a **SOLID**:
Mixing two substances that form a new solid, such as when ice-melting pellets (calcium chloride) combine with baking soda (sodium carbonate) in a solution to create chalk. That is a new solid, called a **PRECIPITATE**.

PRECIPITATE
A new solid that is formed during a chemical reaction.

used to remove laundry stains

CHANGE in **ENERGY**: A chemical reaction that can be in the form of heat and/or light that releases energy.

A physical or chemical reaction that releases heat and energy is **EXOTHERMIC**. An example is making ice cubes.

A physical or chemical reaction that absorbs heat and/or energy to complete its reaction is **ENDOTHERMIC**. For example, boiling water, melting ice cubes.

An experiment that requires boiling an egg produces an example of a chemical change. The liquid yolk and white (clear liquid) inside the egg become solid. That means that new white-and-yellow substances were formed.

CHECK YOUR KNOWLEDGE

1. How is a physical property different from a chemical property?

2. What is the difference between an intensive and extensive property? Give an example of each.

3. If you turn strawberries, blueberries, and yogurt into a smoothie, what change have the ingredients undergone? If you turn eggs, flour, and milk into biscuits, what change have these ingredients undergone?

4. If you burn a wooden log in a campfire, will you have more or less mass than what you started with?

5. Which of the following are NOT considered to be matter: tree, sunlight, grass?

6. Are fireworks an example of an endothermic or exothermic reaction? How do you know?

7. Which of the following is a chemical change and which is a physical change?

A.

C.

BUBBLE BUBBLE

B.

I'M TURNING GREEN!

D.

CHECK YOUR ANSWERS

1. You can see, touch, smell, hear, and detect a physical property without changing the identity. A chemical property becomes evident during or after a chemical reaction.

2. Extensive properties depend on the amount of matter being measured. Intensive properties do NOT depend on the amount of the substance present. Extensive properties are mass, volume, size, weight, and length. Intensive properties are boiling point, density, state of matter, color, melting point, odor, and temperature.

3. The ingredients in the smoothie have undergone a physical change because they are only mixed and could still be separated out. The ingredients in the biscuit will have undergone a chemical change because they have reacted to form a new substance.

4. The burnt log will not have the same mass as the original log. To recover all of the mass of the initial log, you would have to trap the gases that are released during combustion. The mass of the log before burning will equal the mass of the log after burning, plus the mass of the gas that is produced.

5. Sunlight is not matter because it doesn't have substance. A tree and grass are matter because they do have substance. Matter can be measured using mass and volume.

6. Fireworks are an example of an exothermic reaction because they give off heat and light. When burning, the fireworks are hot to the touch.

7. **A.** Physical
   B. Chemical
   C. Physical
   D. Chemical

Chapter 7

STATES OF MATTER

STATES OF MATTER

Matter exists in three main **STATES** (or phases):

- Solid
- Liquid
- Gas (or vapor)

The arrangement of the **MOLECULES** and how they behave determine the state of the substance.

> **MOLECULE**
> Group of atoms bonded together.
>
> **ATOM**
> Small building block or unit of matter.

Atom

Molecule

The molecules within a substance are attracted to one another, which keeps them close. But, each of those molecules has energy associated with how much they move about within the substance. The amount of movement of the molecules and the distance between the molecules within the substance determine its state.

Matter takes the form of these states:

SOLID: Molecules are tightly packed together and don't move about much within the substance.

LIQUID: Molecules are some distance apart and can move about and bump into one another within the substance.

GAS: Molecules are far apart and can move about freely within the substance.

A **SOLID** has a fixed structure, a definite shape. Its shape and volume do not change. Its molecules are packed closely together in a particular pattern and cannot move about freely. Molecules are able to vibrate back and forth in their places, but they cannot break the rigid structure.

Examples: ice, wood, and metal

A **LIQUID** is a substance that flows freely. It does not have a defined shape, but it does have a fixed volume. The energy movement of its molecules causes them to overcome the attractive forces between them. This allows the liquid to take the shape of the container that holds it. Although the particles do move freely, they are still relatively close to one another.

Examples: water, oil, and blood

The speed at which molecules move in a liquid is called **VISCOSITY**. Viscosity is the resistance to flow, sometimes referred to as the **FRICTION** between the molecules of the fluid.

A **GAS** is composed of molecules that are spread far apart. Gas (or vapor) does not have a fixed shape or volume. Its volume and shape are dependent on its container. Unlike a liquid, a gas will expand to fill up the entire container in which it is placed. Gas molecules have relatively HIGH KINETIC ENERGY, which means that they move quickly and are able to overcome the attraction between them and separate.

If you blew up a balloon, and then let it go, the gas inside would immediately spill out and disperse into the air.

Examples: air, steam, and smoke

STATE	Solid	Liquid	Gas
ARRANGEMENT OF PARTICLES			
FEATURES	Fixed shape and volume	Fixed volume; shape can change and flow	Shape and volume not fixed; depends on the container; can flow
MOVEMENT OF PARTICLES	Vibrate, but have fixed positions	Free moving	Move quickly and far apart
COMPRESSIBILITY	Cannot be compressed	Can be compressed, a little	Can be compressed

> **COMPRESSIBILITY**
> Measures the change in volume
> resulting from applied pressure.

PHASE CHANGES

A state of matter is not always permanent. The changes in
temperature or pressure affecting matter are called
PHASE CHANGES. These are phase changes:

MELTING occurs when solid turns into liquid. The
MELTING POINT is the temperature at which the solid
melts. Heat increases the kinetic energy (movement) of
the molecules inside the solid. The increased
energy and movement breaks the
attraction between the molecules and
allows them to move away from one another.

FREEZING is what happens when liquid becomes solid. This
is caused by reducing the temperature. As the temperature
decreases, the molecules inside the liquid have lower kinetic
energy (movement). When the molecules can no longer
overcome their attraction to each other, they form an
ordered structure, or a solid. The point at which a liquid
becomes a solid is called the **FREEZING POINT**.

At standard atmosphere pressure:
Above 100°C, water is a gas (or vapor).
Between 0°C and 100°C, water is a liquid.
Below 0°C, water is a solid.

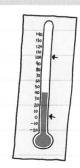

VAPORIZATION occurs when liquid turns to vapor (gas). Vaporization or evaporation happens when molecules break the surface and are in contact with the air.

Sweat is a liquid that forms on your body to regulate your temperature when you are hot. If you don't wipe it off, it will dry. Where did the liquid go? It has absorbed energy from your body and then vaporized, or evaporated, into the air.

When you boil water, some of the liquid turns into steam. That is because the heat increases the kinetic energy of the molecules, and they move faster and then farther apart. The result is vaporization.

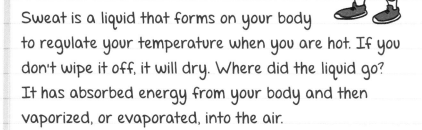

CONDENSATION is the opposite of vaporization—it occurs when gas turns to liquid. When a gas cools, the molecules slow down, attract each other, and then move closer. They stick together and become a liquid. If you place a lid on a pot of boiling water, you would see drops of water form on the inside of the lid. That is condensation. The hot steam hits the colder lid and turns the steam back to liquid.

SUBLIMATION is when a solid becomes a gas, without ever becoming a liquid. That is the important part. Normally, states go from solid to liquid to gas, but sublimation skips a step. Sublimation is rare, because it requires specific conditions to occur, such as the right temperature and pressure. Dry ice sublimes when the solid carbon dioxide (CO_2) turns from ice directly into CO_2 gas.

WHEN A GAS/VAPOR CHANGES TO A SOLID, THAT IS CALLED **DEPOSITION**. FOR EXAMPLE, A DEPOSITION IS FROST ON A COLD WINTER MORNING OR SNOW FORMING WITHIN CLOUDS.

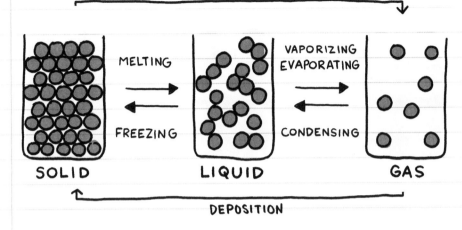

SUBLIMATION

MELTING

FREEZING

SOLID

VAPORIZING
EVAPORATING

CONDENSING

LIQUID

GAS

DEPOSITION

DISPLAYING PHASE CHANGES

A **PHASE DIAGRAM** is a way to show the changes in the state of a substance as it relates to temperature and pressure.

Here is an example of a basic phase diagram. The shape is the same for many substances:

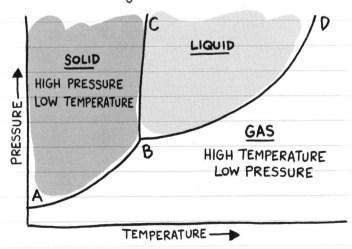

C

D

LIQUID

SOLID

HIGH PRESSURE
LOW TEMPERATURE

GAS

HIGH TEMPERATURE
LOW PRESSURE

B

A

PRESSURE

TEMPERATURE →

A phase diagram is usually set up so that the pressure in atmospheres is plotted against the temperature in degrees Celsius or kelvin. The diagram is divided into three areas representing the solid, liquid, and gaseous states of the substance.

Every point in the diagram indicates a possible combination of temperature and pressure for the substance. The regions separated by the lines show the temperature and pressure that will most likely produce a gas, liquid, or solid. The lines that divide the diagram into states show the temperature and pressure at which two states of the substance are in equilibrium.

HOW TO READ A PHASE DIAGRAM:

An **AB** line represents the rate of *sublimation* (goes up) and *deposition* (goes down). On this line, solid is in equilibrium with gas.

The **BC** line is the rate of *evaporation* (goes up) and *condensation* (goes down). On this line, liquid coexists with gas.

The **BD** line is the rate of *melting* (going up) and *freezing* (going down). On this line, solid coexists with liquid.

Point B is called the **TRIPLE POINT**, where solid, liquid, and gas can all coexist in **EQUILIBRIUM** (together).

Another way of showing what happens during a phase change is to use a **heating** or **cooling curve**. This graph shows the temperature of the substance vs the amount of heat absorbed at constant pressure.

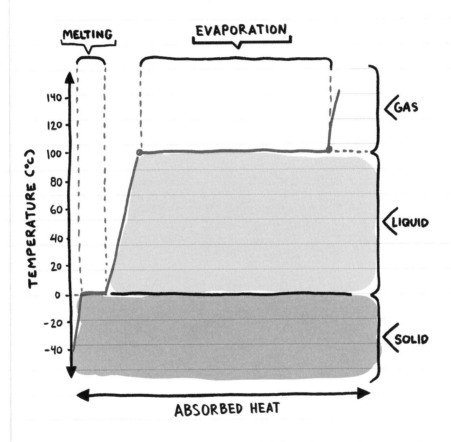

As substances heat, they absorb energy and change state.

A **SOLID** is on the lower left end of the graph. That means that it has low temperature and very little absorbed heat. The graph shows that the temperature of the solid goes from –40°C to 0°C.

But as the heat increases, the red line goes up the graph to the point at which enough energy is absorbed that the substance turns into a **LIQUID**. The range shown on the graph is 0°C to 100°C. When the substance heats up to 100°C, more energy is absorbed, and the substance changes from liquid to **GAS**.

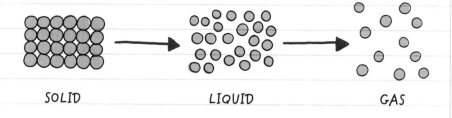

SOLID   LIQUID   GAS

Why does the red line stay flat before it changes state again?

The substance must absorb enough heat so its molecules can move enough to overcome the forces of attraction among them and then change state. All the energy is being put into either the melting or evaporating process and not into any increase in temperature.

CHECK YOUR KNOWLEDGE

1. Name two reasons why a phase change might occur.

2. Do molecules move within a solid?

3. Which of the phases of solid, liquid, and gas are compressible?

4. _____ is the opposite of freezing. _____ is the opposite of condensation. _____ is the opposite of deposition.

5. Name three types of phase changes.

6. In a phase diagram, which two properties are typically plotted against each other on the x- and y-axes?

7. In a heating or cooling curve, what does it mean when the line stays flat for a while before going up or down?

ANSWERS

CHECK YOUR ANSWERS

1. The state of an object is not always permanent. Changes in temperature or pressure affect matter, and these are called phase changes.

2. In a solid, molecules are packed closely together in a particular pattern, and they cannot move about freely. Although the molecules are able to vibrate back and forth in their places, they cannot break the rigid structure.

3. Liquids and gas can be compressed because they don't have a fixed shape. Solids have a fixed shape and cannot be compressed.

4. Melting is the opposite of freezing. Vaporization is the opposite of condensation. Sublimation is the opposite of deposition.

5. Any three of the following: melting, freezing, sublimation, deposition, vaporization, and condensation.

6. A phase diagram is usually set up so that pressure in atmospheres is plotted against temperature in degrees Celsius or Kelvin.

7. The line stays flat in a heating and cooling curve before it changes state, because the substance must absorb enough heat so its molecules can move enough to overcome the forces of attraction.

Chapter 8

ATOMS, ELEMENTS, COMPOUNDS, AND MIXTURES

ATOMS

Matter describes everything that has mass and takes up space. Matter is made up of **ATOMS**.

Atoms are the smallest units of matter that have the properties of a chemical element. Atoms are so small that you can't see them with your eyes or even through a standard laboratory microscope.

Atoms are made up of even smaller (subatomic) particles. Some of these particles have an electrical charge associated with it. A **CHARGE** is a physical property. Charges allow the particles to move through (or remain still in) an electromagnetic field.

Types of Particles

Electrons: Particles with a negative (−) charge

Protons: Particles with a positive (+) charge

Neutrons: Particles have no charge; they are neutral.
There is no notation to indicate a neutral charge.

Protons and neutrons are located in the **NUCLEUS**, or center, of the atom. Because protons have a positive (+) charge and neutrons have no charge, the nucleus has an overall positive charge.

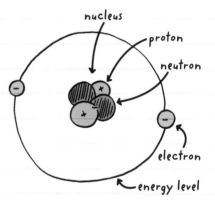

Model of an atom

Electrons occupy "clouds" at certain energy levels and exist at a specific distance from the nucleus.

Electrons, protons, and neutrons are actually not the smallest known particles of matter. There are smaller particles: leptons, muons, tau particles, and quarks.

A **NEUTRAL ATOM** (an atom without an overall charge) will have the same number of protons and electrons. Because the number of electrons (–) is the same as the number of protons (+), the atom has no overall charge.

A **POSITIVE ATOM** (an atom with a positive charge) will have more protons than electrons.

A **NEGATIVE ATOM** (one with a negative charge) will have more electrons than protons.

ELEMENTS AND COMPOUNDS

Atoms are usually classified as elements, also known as pure substances. There are hundreds of atoms.

A **PURE SUBSTANCE** is made up of only one type of atom or one type of molecule. A pure substance can be either an element or a compound. Oxygen, hydrogen, and sodium are all examples of pure substances.

A **MOLECULE** is two or more atoms joining together chemically.

A **COMPOUND** is a molecule that contains at least two different elements (or atoms) that are chemically combined in a fixed ratio.

Water, represented by the chemical symbol H_2O, is a compound because it contains two different elements: hydrogen (H) and oxygen (O).

Table salt, represented by the chemical symbol NaCl, is also a compound because is contains sodium (Na) and chloride (Cl).

A **CHEMICAL SUBSTANCE** is something that can't be separated into its components by physical methods. For example, a diamond starts out as a piece of coal but was subjected to intense heat and pressure. Although it changes form from coal to a diamond, it's still made of the same substance: carbon.

COMPOUNDS AND MIXTURES

A **COMPOUND** is REACTED CHEMICALLY, meaning that each of its individual parts no longer retain their own properties.

FOR EXAMPLE: Sodium (Na) is a highly reactive silverish metal, and chlorine (Cl) is a toxic yellow-green gas at room temperature. But when they combine chemically to become NaCl, the result is table salt, something that you can safely eat every day.

The combinations of the parts of a compound are fixed. Water is always H_2O: one atom of hydrogen (H) and two atoms of oxygen (O).

A **MIXTURE** is made of two or more different substances that are combined. The substances are not chemically bonded, which means that a mixture can be separated into its original parts. An example of a mixture is salad dressing made of oil, vinegar, and maybe herbs or lemon juice.

There are two types of mixtures:

HETEROGENEOUS mixtures contain substances that are not uniform in composition. The parts in the mixture can be separated by physical means.

For example: Pizza is a heterogeneous mixture because every bite contains something different.

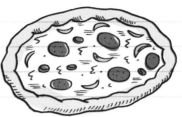

HOMOGENEOUS mixtures are the same throughout and cannot be separated by physical means.

For example: Milk is composed of water, fat, proteins, lactose (the sugar component of milk), and minerals (salts). These substances cannot be separated.

Separating Mixtures

Sometimes you want to separate mixtures so that you can recover their original components. To do that, you must separate them by physical methods.

If you're talking about a pizza, you can just pick off
the pepperoni, sausage, and green peppers.
But you still have the cheese,
sauce, and crust.
Those are more
difficult to separate.

Physical methods used to separate a mixture include:

- Filtration
- Extraction
- Evaporation
- Distillation
- Chromatography

FILTRATION separates an **INSOLUBLE** solid (one that
does not dissolve) from a liquid or solution. A mixture of solid
and liquid solution is poured through a filter, and the solid
collects on the filter paper.

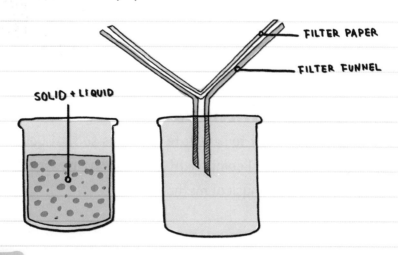

SOLID + LIQUID

FILTER PAPER

FILTER FUNNEL

CHROMATOGRAPHY is a separation process that requires two different phases of matter. It can be used to separate two solids that are mixed to create the same liquid (like the ink in a pen). A thin layer of silica is placed onto a plate. A dot of the liquid being separated is added to the plate. The plate is then placed into a solvent (liquid phase) that slowly moves up the plate (solid phase), separating the parts of the liquid. Chromatography is used to test whether a liquid is a substance or a mixture. It does not separate the entire sample.

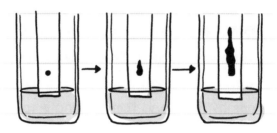

EVAPORATION separates a **SOLUBLE** solid (one that does dissolve, such as table salt) from a liquid, usually water. The solution of the solid and liquid is boiled until the liquid evaporates into the air. The salt is left behind in its original form.

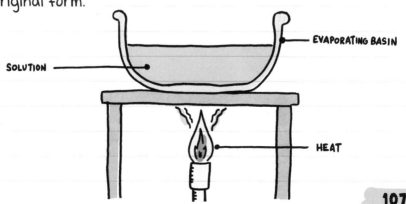

SOLUTION

EVAPORATING BASIN

HEAT

EXTRACTION is the act of isolating one compound from another. The mixture is brought into contact with a solution in which the substance wanted is soluble (will dissolve), but the other substances present are insoluble (won't dissolve).

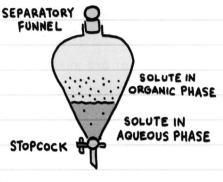

SEPARATORY FUNNEL

SOLUTE IN ORGANIC PHASE

SOLUTE IN AQUEOUS PHASE

STOPCOCK

DISTILLATION is the action of purifying a liquid by the process of heating and cooling. It can be used to separate two liquids that have different boiling points by heating them to evaporate one of them and then cooling it to condense it while the other remains a liquid. This method is mostly used to purify liquids.

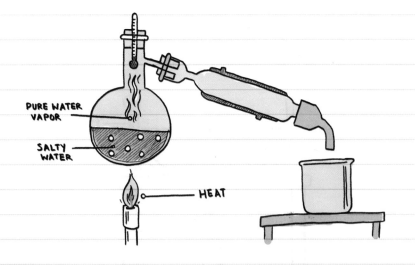

PURE WATER VAPOR

SALTY WATER

HEAT

CHECK YOUR KNOWLEDGE

1. How are matter and atoms related?

2. What are the three basic subatomic particles that make up an atom? Give their charges.

3. Explain the difference between a molecule and a compound.

4. What is the difference between a mixture and a compound?

5. What is the difference between a homogeneous and heterogeneous mixture? Give an example of each.

6. Which two separation methods can be used to separate a solid from a liquid?

7. What is the best way to separate two solids that are mixed to make the same liquid?

ANSWERS

CHECK YOUR ANSWERS

1. Matter is anything that has mass and takes up space, whereas an atom is the smallest unit of matter.

2. The three basic subatomic particles that make up an atom are electrons, protons, and neutrons. Electrons are particles with a negative (–) charge. Protons are particles with a positive (+) charge. Neutrons are particles that have no charge (they are neutral).

3. A molecule is two or more atoms that are chemically joined together. A compound is a molecule that contains at least two different elements (or atoms).

4. A mixture is made of two or more different substances that are mixed together but are not chemically bonded. A compound is mixed chemically, which means that each of its individual parts no longer retains its own properties.

5. A heterogeneous mixture is one in which the substances are not evenly mixed and can still be separated, for example, pizza. A homogeneous mixture is a mixture that is the same throughout, for example, milk.

6. Two methods that can be used to separate a solid from a liquid are filtration and distillation.

7. Chromatography is the best method for separating two solids that are mixed to make the same liquid.

Unit 3

Atomic Theory and Electron Configuration

Chapter 9

ATOMIC THEORY

THEORY DEVELOPMENT

John Dalton

JOHN DALTON was the first scientist to develop an atomic theory based on scientific observation. He believed that:

> **John Dalton** was an English scientist. He is often referred to as the father of atomic theory. In 1803, he proposed the theory of the atom.

■ All matter is made of atoms.

■ Atoms cannot be broken down further.

■ Atoms within an element are the same; atoms from different elements are not.

For example, hydrogen atoms (H) are different from oxygen atoms (O).

■ Atoms are rearranged during a chemical reaction, but are not lost (the LAW OF CONSERVATION OF MASS).

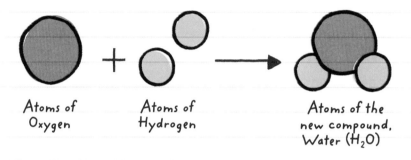

Atoms of
Oxygen

Atoms of
Hydrogen

Atoms of the
new compound,
Water (H_2O)

Compounds are formed when atoms from two or more elements combine. In any one compound, the ratio of the number of atoms to one another is a whole number (LAW OF MULTIPLE PROPORTIONS).

For example, in CO_2, the ratio of carbon to oxygen atoms is 1:2.

carbon (C)   oxygen (O)

The **Law of Multiple Proportions** states that if two elements combine to form more than one compound, the masses of one element will combine with the other element in a whole-number ratio.

Dalton's theory didn't get everything right. For example, it was later confirmed that atoms can be broken down into subatomic particles (known as electrons, neutrons, and protons), but it was a great start because atoms and molecules are still the smallest particles a substance can be and still retain its chemical and physical properties.

J. J. Thomson

Part of Dalton's theory was disproved when SIR JOSEPH JOHN (J. J.) THOMSON discovered the electron in 1897. Thomson used the idea of **RADIATION**, energy that is transmitted in the form of waves, particles, or rays.

> **J. J. Thomson** was an English physicist who is credited with the discovery of the electron and proposed the "plum pudding" model of the atom.

Using electromagnetic radiation theory, Thomson built a CATHODE RAY TUBE to prove that negatively charged particles (electrons) were present in atoms.

A **cathode ray tube** is a closed glass cylinder in which most of the air has been removed. Inside the tube are two **ELECTRODES**, a **CATHODE**, which is the negatively charged electrode, and an **ANODE**, which is the positively charged electrode.

A neon sign is a cathode ray tube.

When a high voltage is applied between the electrodes, a beam of electrons travels from the anode to the cathode. Thomson was able to determine the ratio of electric charge to the mass of a single electron. That number is

$$-1.76 \times 10^8 \text{ Coulomb (C)/g.}$$

the unit of electric charge

Thomson imagined that atoms looked like a "bowl of plum pudding," meaning the electrons just "sat" in a pudding of protons. The negative charges of the electrons were canceled out by the positive charges of the protons.

J. J. Thomson believed that electrons were like plums inside a positively charged "pudding."

Ernest Rutherford

ERNEST RUTHERFORD, a British physicist, took Thomson's idea a step further by using radioactive particles. He shot positively charged ALPHA PARTICLES (particles made up of two protons and two neutrons) through a piece of gold foil. He noticed that some of the alpha particles went straight through the foil, but others bounced back. What would cause the alpha particles to bounce back? Rutherford theorized that:

- Atoms are made of mostly empty space (which is why most particles went "straight through" the gold foil).

- Atoms have a positively charged center (which caused the positively charged particles to "bounce back").

His second idea came from the theory that because "like repels like" (meaning positive charges repel positive charges), the positively charged alpha particles were most likely hitting the center of the atom, which was also positively charged. He named that center of the atom the **NUCLEUS**.

> **NUCLEUS**
> Positively charged central core of an atom; contains nearly all of its mass.

DEVELOPMENT OF THEORY OF ELECTRON CHARGES

Electrons are matter. All matter has mass; therefore, electrons must have mass. But how do you measure the mass of something as small as an electron?

R. A. Millikan

In 1909, R. A. MILLIKAN performed an experiment in which he was able to find the size of the charge on an electron.

> **Robert Andrews Millikan**
> was an American physicist who received the Nobel Prize in Physics in 1923 for his work on measurement of the elementary electric charge.

MILLIKAN OIL-DROP EXPERIMENT

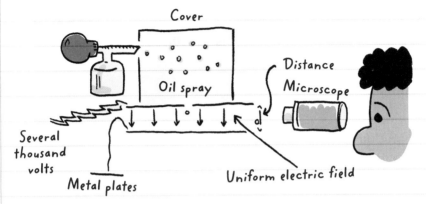

Millikan placed a negative charge onto a drop of oil. He then determined how much electric charge must be applied to suspend the oil drop in an electronic field between two metal plates. By balancing the gravitational and electric forces on the oil drop, he could determine the charge. After multiple experiments, he found that the charge on an electron was -1.602×10^{-19} C.

Using Thomson's charge/mass ratio of the electron, Millikan determined the mass of an electron.

$$\text{Mass of an electron} = \frac{\text{charge}}{\text{charge/mass}} = \frac{1.6022}{-1.76} \times \frac{10^{-19}}{10^{8}} = 9.10 \times 10^{-28} \text{ g}$$

The charge of both the electron and proton, known as the **ELEMENTARY ELECTRIC CHARGE (E) OR (Q)**, is -1.6022×10^{-1} C.

Because Rutherford knew the charge of the proton, he could plug it into his equation and calculate it in reverse to determine that **the mass of the proton is** -1.672×10^{-27} **kg**.

James Chadwick

JAMES CHADWICK spent his life studying the nucleus of the Rutherford atom and found the mass of the nucleus to be twice as large as previously thought. In addition, Chadwick noticed that the

> **James Chadwick** was a British physicist who discovered the neutron in 1932. He was awarded the Nobel Prize in Physics in 1935.

Rutherford atom was neutral, yet the protons had a positive charge. These pieces of information led Chadwick to theorize that there must be small particles other than protons present in an atom's nucleus: ones without a charge. He named these subatomic particles **NEUTRONS**.

Measured masses and charges of the three elementary particles		
PARTICLE	CHARGE (C)	MASS (kg)
Electron	-1.60×10^{-19}	9.1×10^{-31}
Proton	1.60×10^{-19}	1.672×10^{-27}
Neutron	0.00	1.674×10^{-27}

CHECK YOUR KNOWLEDGE

1. Who was the first scientist to develop the atomic theory?

2. True or false: The atoms in sodium (Na) are different from the atoms in chlorine (Cl).

3. Explain the difference between a cathode and an anode.

4. Which scientist built a cathode ray tube to prove that negatively charged particles (electrons) and positively charged particles (protons) were present in atoms?

5. What experiment did Rutherford perform with regard to atomic structure? What did his research prove?

6. Does the nucleus of an atom have a charge? If so, what is it?

7. Who determined the charge of an electron?

ANSWERS

CHECK YOUR ANSWERS

1. John Dalton

2. True. They have different numbers of protons, neutrons, and electrons.

3. A cathode is a negatively charged electrode, and an anode is a positively charged electrode.

4. J.J. Thomson

5. Rutherford shot an alpha ray through a piece of gold foil. He noticed that some of the rays went straight through the foil, which was expected, but others bounced back. He proved that every atom has a nucleus.

6. Yes. The charge is positive.

7. Millikan, with his oil-drop experiment

Chapter 10

WAVES, QUANTUM THEORY, AND PHOTONS

WHAT IS A WAVE?

A **WAVE** is a vibrating disturbance through which energy is transmitted. Waves are described by their height and length, which are measured by **AMPLITUDE** and **FREQUENCY**.

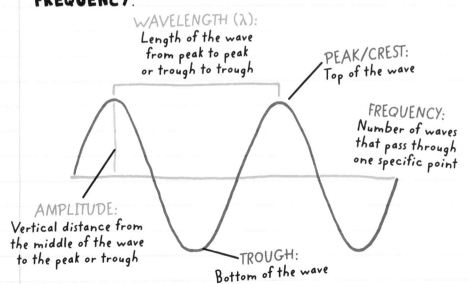

WAVELENGTH (λ):
Length of the wave from peak to peak or trough to trough

PEAK/CREST:
Top of the wave

FREQUENCY:
Number of waves that pass through one specific point

AMPLITUDE:
Vertical distance from the middle of the wave to the peak or trough

TROUGH:
Bottom of the wave

HUH?!

The units of measurement for a wavelength vary. They can be measured in meters, centimeters, nanometers, or Ångströms.

An Ångström is a unit of length equal to 10^{-10} meter, or one-hundred millionth of a centimeter.

THE ELECTROMAGNETIC SPECTRUM

Up until 1900, scientists believed that the energy of an electron acted like a wave, meaning it was able to move up and down. An example of this motion was found in **ELECTROMAGNETIC (EM) RADIATION**.

EM radiation is all around us and takes many forms. Most of the wavelengths and frequencies of EM radiation are invisible to the naked eye. Examples of common EM radiation are:

Rays from the sun

Flame from a burning fire

X-rays

The collection of all types of EM radiation is called the **EM SPECTRUM**. The EM spectrum has seven different parts:

- radio
- microwave
- infrared
- visible
- ultraviolet
- X-ray
- gamma ray

The visible light spectrum from low to high energy can be memorized using this mnemonic:

Roger **M**akes **I**nstruments: **V**iolins, **U**kuleles, **X**ylophones, and **G**uitars.

(**R**adio, **M**icrowaves, **I**nfrared, **V**isible, **U**ltraviolet, **X**-rays, **G**amma rays)

Humans can only see one small part of the EM spectrum and that is the **visible spectrum**. This rainbow-colored portion is made up of the colors that humans can see: red, orange, yellow, green, blue, indigo, and violet. The arrow and scale show that the color violet has a short wavelength and higher frequency, and the color red has a longer wavelength and a shorter frequency.

The colors arranged in order from longest to shortest wavelengths are: Red, Orange, Yellow, Green, Blue, Indigo, and Violet, also represented by their acronym, ROYGBIV.

The Electromagnetic Spectrum

Wavelength (meters)	About the size of:
RADIO ← 1	Buildings
MICROWAVE 1 to 10^{-3}	Grains of sugar
INFARED 10^{-3} to 7×10^{-7}	Protozoan
VISIBLE 7×10^{-7} to 4×10^{-7}	Bacteria
ULTRAVIOLET 3×10^{-7} to 10^{-8}	Molecules
X-RAY 10^{-8} to 10^{-12}	Atoms
GAMMA RAY 10^{-12} ⟶	Atomic nuclei

The positioning on the chart indicates the size of each type of wave. A radio wave is long and wide, like a jump rope that is being waved up and down. A gamma ray is tiny, like the nucleus of an atom.

When you watch TV, listen to the radio, or use a microwave, you are using EM waves.

PLANCK'S THEORY

German physicist MAX PLANCK discovered that electrons can also act like particles, because when they hit a metal surface they emit electrons. Planck heated solids until they glowed red hot and then observed that they emitted EM radiation. He found that EM radiation was emitted in small packages. He called these packages **QUANTA** (singular: **quantum**).

A **QUANTUM** is the smallest quantity of energy that can be emitted or absorbed in the form of EM energy.

Simple explanation: Every day, you deal with things in specific quantities. If you want to buy a candy bar, it costs 89 cents ($.89). With a tax of 7%, you would owe $0.0623, or about $6\frac{1}{4}$ cents in tax. But you can't give someone $\frac{1}{4}$ of a penny.

A quantum is like a penny. A penny is the smallest cash coin available in the U.S. You cannot give someone half of a penny. You also can't have any unit of energy smaller than a quantum.

What is a quantum "worth"?

Planck measured the energy of a quantum with this equation:

$$\epsilon = h\nu$$

where **h** is Planck's constant at **6.626×10^{-34} Joules (J)/s**, and **v** is the frequency of the light absorbed or emitted.

Planck's constant relates the energy in 1 quantum of EM radiation to the frequency of that radiation.

> A joule is an SI unit of energy.

OR, if you are using the speed of light, **c**, the equation for a quantum can look like this:

$$\epsilon = \frac{hc}{\lambda},$$

> λ is called **lambda**
>
> λ = wavelength

because $\nu = c/\lambda$

The speed of light $c = 3 \times 10^8$ m/s.

Quantum theory is the study of matter and energy on the atomic and subatomic levels. Quantum theory allows scientists to understand how electrons behave and to make predictions.

Important! According to quantum theory, energy is always emitted in whole-number multiples of $h\nu$; for example, $h\nu$, $2\ h\nu$, and $3\ h\nu$, but not $1.96\ h\nu$ or $3.2\ h\nu$.

THE PHOTON

ALBERT EINSTEIN took Planck's theory to the next level. Einstein shot a beam of light onto a metal surface, which caused electrons to be emitted. This emission is called the **PHOTOELECTRIC EFFECT**. Einstein found that

Albert Einstein was a German physicist who developed the theory of relativity. He was awarded the Nobel Prize in Physics in 1921 for his discovery of the Law of Photoelectric Effect.

the number of electrons that were ejected from the metal was proportional to the brightness of the light.

Photoelectric effect:

Brighter light = more electrons ejected

However, the energy of the light must be above a certain frequency (called the THRESHOLD FREQUENCY) for electrons to be ejected. If the energy is below the threshold frequency, none of the electrons will be ejected.

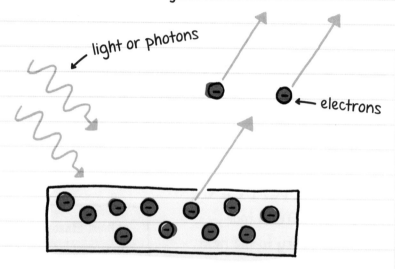

light or photons

electrons

The box contains free-floating electrons. As the energy in the form of light enters the box, it pushes out electrons.

In other words, electrons inside metal atoms are held together tightly, so it takes a lot of light to push an electron out. If the light doesn't have enough oomph (or isn't a high enough frequency) it can't make the electron budge.

Imagine that you are holding on to a basketball as tightly as you can with two hands. Another person wants to push the basketball out of your grip. That means that they must apply a lot of force to get you to let go of the ball. If they push at the ball lightly, you keep holding on to the basketball.

But if they push hard enough, they can knock it out of your hands.

That basketball represents the electron. The hard push represents a beam of energy that is above the threshold frequency.

Einstein suggested that the beam of light that could eject an electron was a *particle* of light called a **PROTON**.

He said that photons possess energy ε, which is given by the equation:

$$\varepsilon = h\nu \quad \text{OR} \quad \varepsilon = \frac{hc}{\lambda}$$

where c is the speed of light, and c = 3 × 10⁸ m/s.

> Energy is equal to the wavelength multiplied by the frequency of light absorbed or emitted.

So that means:

A photon = a quantum

Photons are the smallest unit of energy (like a quantum) and have the following characteristics:

- They are neutral and stable and have no mass.

- They interact with electrons and have energy and speed that is dependent on their frequency.

- They can travel at the speed of light, but only in a vacuum, such as space.

- All light and EM energy are made of photons.

CHECK YOUR KNOWLEDGE

1. What is quantum theory?

2. Why is it important to study quantum theory?

3. What are the three properties that you can measure in a wave?

4. Can a partial photon be emitted from an object?

5. Is a photon the same as an electron?

6. What are three characteristics of photons?

ANSWERS ⟩ 133

CHECK YOUR ANSWERS

1. Quantum theory explains the behavior of matter and energy on atomic and subatomic levels.

2. Quantum theory allows scientists to predict and understand how electrons will behave.

3. The three properties you can measure in a wave are amplitude, frequency, and wavelength.

4. A partial photon cannot be emitted from an object because photons are only emitted in whole numbers, such as 1, 2, 3, etc.

5. No, photons differ from electrons because a photon is the smallest unit of energy, like a quantum. Photons are massless.

6. Photons are neutral, stable, and have no mass. They interact with electrons and have energy and speed that is dependent on their frequency. They can travel at the speed of light, but only in a vacuum, such as space. All light and EM energy is made of photons.

Unit 4

Elements and the Periodic Table

Chapter 11

THE PERIODIC TABLE

Different types of atoms are called **ELEMENTS**.

- Elements are unique and are made of one type of atom.

- There are 118 known elements.

- Elements can have different numbers of protons and electrons. This explains all of the differences in the physical properties of matter.

- Some elements exist at room temperature as a gas, some are liquid, and some are solid.

All elements are listed and organized in a chart called the **PERIODIC TABLE**.

Dmitri Ivanovich Mendeleev was a Russian scientist who invented the periodic table in 1869.

The periodic table is arranged in a grid format. Each element sits in a specific place in the grid, according to its **ATOMIC NUMBER**. The number of protons in an element defines its position in the periodic table, according to modern periodic law.

ATOMIC NUMBER
The number of protons that an atom contains.

also the number of electrons

STRUCTURE OF THE PERIODIC TABLE

The periodic table contains three major categories of elements:

Metals are positioned to the left of the table, **metalloids** are in the middle, and **nonmetals** are positioned to the right.

Each element on the periodic table is assigned a **CHEMICAL SYMBOL**, which is one or two letters long. The first letter is always uppercase and the second letter (if there is one) is lowercase. For example:

Sodium = Na
Magnesium = Mg
Sulfur = S

THE PERIODIC TABLE

← PERIOD →

Atomic Number — 3
Chemical Symbol — Li
Element Name — Lithium
Average Atomic Mass — 6.941

↑ GROUP ↓

1								
1 H Hydrogen 1.0078	2							
3 Li Lithium 6.941	4 Be Beryllium 9.0122							
11 Na Sodium 22.990	12 Mg Magnesium 24.305	3	4	5	6	7	8	9
19 K Potassium 39.098	20 Ca Calcium 40.078	21 Sc Scandium 44.956	22 Ti Titanium 47.867	23 V Vanadium 50.942	24 Cr Chromium 51.996	25 Mn Manganese 54.938	26 Fe Iron 55.845	27 Co Cobalt 58.933
37 Rb Rubidium 85.468	38 Sr Strontium 87.62	39 Y Yttrium 88.906	40 Zr Zirconium 91.224	41 Nb Niobium 92.906	42 Mo Molybdenum 95.95	43 Tc Technetium 98.9062	44 Ru Ruthenium 101.07	45 Rh Rhodium 102.91
55 Cs Caesium 132.91	56 Ba Barium 137.33		72 Hf Hafnium 178.49	73 Ta Tantalum 180.95	74 W Tungsten 183.84	75 Re Rhenium 186.21	76 Os Osmium 190.23	77 Ir Iridium 192.22
87 Fr Francium (223)	88 Ra Radium (226)		104 Rf Rutherfordium (267)	105 Db Dubnium (268)	106 Sg Seaborgium (269)	107 Bh Bohrium (264)	108 Hs Hassium (269)	109 Mt Meitnerium (278)

57 La Lanthanum 138.91	58 Ce Cerium 140.12	59 Pr Praseodymium 140.91	60 Nd Neodymium 144.24	61 Pm Promethium (145)	62 Sm Samarium 150.36
89 Ac Actinium (226)	90 Th Thorium 232.04	91 Pa Protactinium 231.04	92 U Uranium 238.03	93 Np Neptunium (237)	94 Pu Plutonium (244)

→ ALKALI METALS

→ ALKALINE EARTH METALS

→ LANTHANIDES

→ ACTINIDES

→ TRANSITION METALS

→ UNKNOWN PROPERTIES

→ POST-TRANSITION METALS

→ METALLOIDS

→ OTHER NONMETALS

→ HALOGENS

→ NOBLE GASES

→ NEW AND PENDING DISCOVERIES

13	14	15	16	17	18
					2 He Helium 4.0026
5 B Boron 10.806	6 C Carbon 12.009	7 N Nitrogen 14.006	8 O Oxygen 15.999	9 F Fluorine 18.998	10 Ne Neon 20.180
13 Al Aluminum 26.982	14 Si Silicon 28.084	15 P Phosphorus 30.974	16 S Sulfur 32.059	17 Cl Chlorine 35.446	18 Ar Argon 39.948

10	11	12	13	14	15	16	17	18
28 Ni Nickel 58.693	29 Cu Copper 63.546	30 Zn Zinc 65.38	31 Ga Gallium 69.723	32 Ge Germanium 72.63	33 As Arsenic 74.922	34 Se Selenium 78.96	35 Br Bromine 79.904	36 Kr Krypton 83.798
46 Pd Palladium 106.42	47 Ag Silver 107.87	48 Cd Cadmium 112.41	49 In Indium 114.82	50 Sn Tin 118.71	51 Sb Antimony 121.76	52 Te Tellurium 127.60	53 I Iodine 126.90	54 Xe Xenon 131.29
78 Pt Platinum 195.08	79 Au Gold 196.97	80 Hg Mercury 200.59	81 Tl Thallium 204.38	82 Pb Lead 207.2	83 Bi Bismuth 208.98	84 Po Polonium (209)	85 At Astatine (210)	86 Rn Radon (222)
110 Ds Darmstadtium (281)	111 Rg Roentgenium (281)	112 Cn Copernicium (285)	113 Nh Nihonium (286)	114 Fl Flerovium (289)	115 Mc Moscovium (289)	116 Lv Livermorium (293)	117 Tn Tennessine (294)	118 Og Oganesson (294)

63 Eu Europium 151.96	64 Gd Gadolinium 157.25	65 Tb Terbium 158.93	66 Dy Dysprosium 162.50	67 Ho Holmium 164.93	68 Er Erbium 167.26	69 Tm Thulium 168.93	70 Yb Ytterbium 173.04	71 Lu Lutetium 174.97
95 Am Americium (243)	96 Cm Curium (247)	97 Bk Berkelium (247)	98 Cf Californium (251)	99 Es Einsteinium (252)	100 Fm Fermium (257)	101 Md Mendelevium (258)	102 No Nobelium (259)	103 Lr Lawrencium (262)

In many cases, the letters in a chemical symbol correspond to the name of the element. . . . But not always.

For example:

Oxygen is **O**
Zinc is **Zn**
but **Lead** is **Pb**

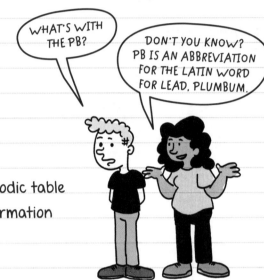

WHAT'S WITH THE PB?

DON'T YOU KNOW? PB IS AN ABBREVIATION FOR THE LATIN WORD FOR LEAD, PLUMBUM.

Each square in the periodic table contains the same information about the element:

- Atomic number
- Chemical symbol
- Element name
- Average atomic mass

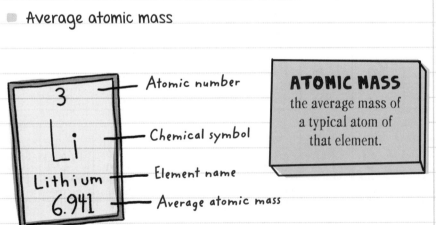

3
Li
Lithium
6.941

— Atomic number
— Chemical symbol
— Element name
— Average atomic mass

ATOMIC MASS
the average mass of a typical atom of that element.

The periodic table is organized by rows and columns. A horizontal row is called a **PERIOD**. A vertical column is called a **GROUP** or **FAMILY**. The structure of the table is based on mass.

PERIOD
the row of elements *across* the periodic table (horizontal).

The elements are arranged from left to right by increasing atomic number. As you go across from left to right, each element has one more electron and one more proton than the element to the left of it.

GROUP or **FAMILY**
a column of elements in the periodic table. Groups have similar physical and chemical properties.

FOR EXAMPLE: Hydrogen (H) has one electron, helium (He) has two electrons, lithium (Li) has three electrons, and so on. Elements in the same column have similar physical and chemical properties.

NEUTRAL ELEMENTS, ISOTOPES, AND IONS

In a **NEUTRAL ELEMENT**, the number of protons equals the number of electrons. This means that the element has a charge of 0.

The atomic number tells you the number of protons. If the element is neutral, it also tells you the number of electrons.

To find the number of neutrons, subtract the atomic number from the mass number (average atomic mass rounded to the nearest whole number).

$$\text{mass number} - \text{atomic number} = \text{number of neutrons}$$

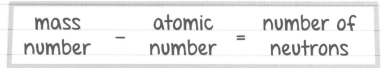

20 ← Atomic number

Ca

Calcium

40.08 ← Average atomic mass

40.08 = 40 ← (round the atomic mass to the nearest whole number)

40 - 20 = 20 ← (subtract the atomic number from the mass number)

Calcium has 20 neutrons. It is a neutral element.

COMMON ELEMENTS

We use a number of elements on the periodic table every day.

For example:

ALUMINUM (AL) is used in making planes, pots, and pans.

GOLD (AU) is used to make jewelry, and diamonds are composed of carbon (C).

SODIUM (NA) is combined with chlorine (Cl) to make table salt.

NEON (NE) is used to make neon signs.

IRON (FE) is used to make steel girders for bridges or buildings.

ISOTOPES

ISOTOPES are atoms of the same element. For example, carbon-14 is an isotope of carbon. Isotopes always have the same number of protons with different atomic masses.

> More neutrons = more mass = heavier atoms
>
> Fewer neutrons = less mass = lighter atoms

> The atomic mass is included in the information for each element in the periodic table.

Each isotope of an element is identified with a **MASS NUMBER**, which is the sum of the atomic number (number of protons) and neutrons in the nucleus.

> Mass number = atomic number + number of neutrons

To write an isotope, you must know:

- the mass number
- atomic number
- element symbol
- charge (if it has one)

The format looks like this:

$$^{\text{mass number}}_{\text{atomic number}} \text{(element symbol)}^{\text{charge}}$$

FOR EXAMPLE: Carbon-14 has six protons and eight neutrons.

More neutrons = more mass = heavier atoms

The isotope is written like this:

mass number →

$$^{14}_{6}\text{C}$$ ← element symbol

atomic number →

Carbon-14 has no charge, so there is no symbol next to the element symbol or number.

FOR EXAMPLE: An oxygen isotope, O^{2-} is written as

$$^{14}_{6}\text{O}^{2-}$$

The isotope has a -2 charge.

> If a charge is +1 or -1 we write + or - (without the 1) as the superscript.

Hydrogen has three isotopes:

Protium has one proton and is the stable atom of hydrogen.
It is written as

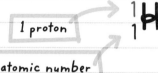

^1_1H

1 proton

atomic number

Deuterium has one proton and one neutron and is an isotope
written as

1 proton + 1 neutron → ^2_1H

Tritium has one proton and two neutrons and is an isotope
written as

1 proton + 2 neutrons → ^3_1H

A model of hydrogen's isotopes would look like this:

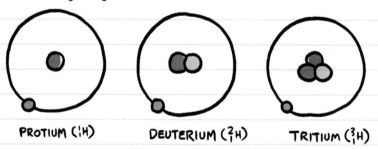

PROTIUM (^1_1H)   DEUTERIUM (^2_1H)   TRITIUM (^3_1H)

Isotopes are used in:

SMOKE DETECTORS: The
americium-241 isotope initiates a small
current that, when interrupted by
smoke, causes the detector to go off.

NUCLEAR REACTORS: The isotope
U-235 is used in nuclear reactors
because under certain conditions, it
can split and give off a large amount
of energy.

BATTERIES IN NASA SPACECRAFT:
Isotope plutonium-238 is used for
batteries to power long-term space
travel. As plutonium-238 decays, it gives
off heat that is converted to energy.

IONS

If an atom has a charge it is called an **ION**.

A negatively charged ion (-), or **ANION**, results when
an atom gains one or more electrons.

A positively charged ion (+), or **CATION**, results when an atom loses or gives away one or more electrons.

Think: Cat + Iron

− and + changes attract.
− and − changes repel.
+ and + changes repel.

THIS IS OFTEN SUMMED UP AS "LIKE REPELS LIKE"

A positive ion, or cation, will be attracted to a negative ion, or an anion.

A positive ion will be repelled by another positive ion.

A negative ion will be repelled by another negative ion.

Ions with different charges and their attractions:

attraction

repulsion

neutral

no attraction, no repulsion

CHECK YOUR KNOWLEDGE

1. How many known elements are there?

2. Which number on the periodic table tells the number of protons in an element?

3. What is the name of a row across the periodic table? What is the name of a vertical column in the periodic table?

4. Who is known as the father of the periodic table? On what measurement did he base his structure of the periodic table?

5. What is the difference between atomic number and atomic mass? Why is this difference so important to the periodic table?

6. What is the difference between an anion and a cation? Give examples of each.

ANSWERS

CHECK YOUR ANSWERS

1. There are 118 known elements.

2. The atomic number tells you the number of protons in an element.

3. A row in the periodic table is called a period. A column is called a group or a family.

4. Dmitri Mendeleev is known as the father of the periodic table. He based the structure of the elements on mass.

5. Atomic number is the number of protons that an atom contains. Atomic mass is the weighted average based on relative abundance of isotopes. Henry Moseley, a British chemist, reorganized Mendeleev's table by atomic number, not atomic mass. Everything "fell" into place. Moseley determined that atomic number increases in the same order as atomic mass.

6. An anion is a negatively charged ion. A cation is a positively charged ion. Examples of anions are: chloride, nitrite, sulfate, and phosphate. Examples of cations are: lithium, sodium, and potassium.

Chapter 12

PERIODIC TRENDS

TYPES OF ELEMENTS

The periodic table is governed by **PERIODIC LAW**, which states:

Physical and chemical properties of the elements recur in a systematic and predictable way when the elements are arranged in order of increasing atomic number.

Periodic law is considered to be one of the most important concepts in chemistry. It helps chemists to predict how an element will behave.

If you know an element's position on the periodic table, you can predict its properties.

Elements in the periodic table are split up into three categories:

METALS   **NONMETALS**   **METALLOIDS**

METALS are:

- Solid at room temperature (except for mercury [Hg], which is a liquid at room temperature)

- **DUCTILE** (can be pulled into thin wires)

- **LUSTROUS** (or "high luster"/shiny)

- Good conductors of electricity and heat

- **MALLEABLE** (can be hammered into thin sheets)

- Prone to lose electrons easily

NONMETALS have properties that are *opposite* from those in metals. They are:

- **BRITTLE**

- Dull or not shiny

- Poor conductors of electricity and heat

- Solid, liquid, or gaseous at room temperature

- Able to gain or share electrons easily

METALLOIDS have properties that are a *mix* of metal and nonmetal properties. They are:

- Solid at room temperature

- Dull or shiny

- A mix of good conductors and poor conductors of electricity and heat

- Characterized by having physical properties that tend to be metallic and chemical properties that tend to be nonmetallic

Periodic table showing the three categories

→ METAL
→ METALLOID
→ NONMETAL

1 H Hydrogen 1.0078

3 Li Lithium 6.941	4 Be Beryllium 9.0122

11 Na Sodium 22.990	12 Mg Magnesium 24.305

19 K Potassium 39.098	20 Ca Calcium 40.078	21 Sc Scandium 44.956	22 Ti Titanium 47.867	23 V Vanadium 50.942	24 Cr Chromium 51.996	25 Mn Manganese 54.938	26 Fe Iron 55.845	27 Co Cobalt 58.933
37 Rb Rubidium 85.468	38 Sr Strontium 87.62	39 Y Yttrium 88.906	40 Zr Zirconium 91.224	41 Nb Niobium 92.906	42 Mo Molybdenum 95.95	43 Tc Technetium 98.9062	44 Ru Ruthenium 101.07	45 Rh Rhodium 102.91
55 Cs Caesium 132.91	56 Ba Barium 137.33		72 Hf Hafnium 178.49	73 Ta Tantalum 180.95	74 W Tungsten 183.84	75 Re Rhenium 186.21	76 Os Osmium 190.23	77 Ir Iridium 192.22
87 Fr Francium (223)	88 Ra Radium (226)		104 Rf Rutherfordium (267)	105 Db Dubnium (268)	106 Sg Seaborgium (269)	107 Bh Bohrium (264)	108 Hs Hassium (269)	109 Mt Meitnerium (278)

57 La Lanthanum 138.91	58 Ce Cerium 140.12	59 Pr Praseodymium 140.91	60 Nd Neodymium 144.24	61 Pm Promethium (145)	62 Sm Samarium 150.36
89 Ac Actinium (226)	90 Th Thorium 232.04	91 Pa Protactinium 231.04	92 U Uranium 238.03	93 Np Neptunium (237)	94 Pu Plutonium (244)

						2 He Helium 4.0026
5 B Boron 10.806	6 C Carbon 12.009	7 N Nitrogen 14.006	8 O Oxygen 15.999	9 F Fluorine 18.998	10 Ne Neon 20.180
13 Al Aluminum 26.982	14 Si Silicon 28.084	15 P Phosphorus 30.974	16 S Sulfur 32.059	17 Cl Chlorine 35.446	18 Ar Argon 39.948

28 Ni Nickel 58.693	29 Cu Copper 63.546	30 Zn Zinc 65.38	31 Ga Gallium 69.723	32 Ge Germanium 72.63	33 As Arsenic 74.922	34 Se Selenium 78.96	35 Br Bromine 79.904	36 Kr Krypton 83.798
46 Pd Palladium 106.42	47 Ag Silver 107.87	48 Cd Cadmium 112.41	49 In Indium 114.82	50 Sn Tin 118.71	51 Sb Antimony 121.76	52 Te Tellurium 127.60	53 I Iodine 126.90	54 Xe Xenon 131.29
78 Pt Platinum 195.08	79 Au Gold 196.97	80 Hg Mercury 200.59	81 Tl Thallium 204.38	82 Pb Lead 207.2	83 Bi Bismuth 208.98	84 Po Polonium (209)	85 At Astatine (210)	86 Rn Radon (222)
110 Ds Darmstadtium (281)	111 Rg Roentgenium (281)	112 Cn Copernicium (285)	113 Nh Nihonium (286)	114 Fl Flerovium (289)	115 Mc Moscovium (289)	116 Lv Livermorium (293)	117 Tn Tennessine (294)	118 Og Oganesson (294)

63 Eu Europium 151.96	64 Gd Gadolinium 157.25	65 Tb Terbium 158.93	66 Dy Dysprosium 162.50	67 Ho Holmium 164.93	68 Er Erbium 167.26	69 Tm Thulium 168.93	70 Yb Ytterbium 173.04	71 Lu Lutetium 174.97
95 Am Americium (243)	96 Cm Curium (247)	97 Bk Berkelium (247)	98 Cf Californium (251)	99 Es Einsteinium (252)	100 Fm Fermium (257)	101 Md Mendelevium (258)	102 No Nobelium (259)	103 Lr Lawrencium (262)

FAMILIES IN THE PERIODIC TABLE

A family (or group) in the periodic table is a set of elements that share the same properties. The characteristics of each element's display is determined by the number of **VALENCE ELECTRONS**. Valence electrons decide how an atom will react in a chemical reaction.

> **VALENCE ELECTRON**
> An electron located in the outermost shell.

Every element wants to have a **FULL OCTET**, which is typically, but not always, eight electrons in the outer shell. To get a full octet, an element will gain or lose valence electrons, the electrons in the outermost shell.

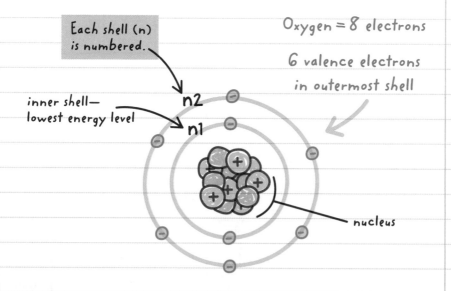

Each shell (n) is numbered.

inner shell— lowest energy level

n2

n1

Oxygen = 8 electrons

6 valence electrons in outermost shell

nucleus

The OCTET RULE says that elements must combine in such a way that each atom has eight electrons in its valence shell, so that it has the same electronic configuration as a noble gas.

There are five major groups in the periodic table:

Alkali Metals: Group 1 (IA)

Each group is numbered.

Alkaline Earth Metals: Group 2 (IIA)

Transition Metals: Groups 3-12

Halogens: Group 17 (VIIA)

Noble Gases: Group 18 (VIIIA)

Groups 13-16 contain **metalloids**. Metalloids are the smallest group. Unlike the major groups, metalloids contain two categories: metals and nonmetals.

ALKALI METALS
Elements in this group have the following properties:

- Have one valence electron that they will give up easily to get an octet, so that the ion has a 1+ charge

- Are soft, metallic solids that are also shiny

- Are good heat and electrical conductors

- Have low densities and relatively low melting points, decreasing with atomic mass

ALKALINE EARTH METALS
Elements in this group have the following properties:

- Contain two valence electrons that they will give up, so that the ion has a 2+ charge

- Are metallic solids, which are harder than alkali metals

- Are more dense, have higher melting points, and are better conductors than alkali metals

TRANSITION METALS
Elements in this group have the following properties:

- The number of electrons that they can lose varies; multiple charges are possible

- Are hard metallic solids, very good conductors, and have high melting points

- Are shiny, dense, and lustrous

HALOGENS
Elements in this group have the following properties:

- Have seven valence electrons and want to gain an electron

- Are reactive nonmetals

- Have melting points and boiling points that increase as the atomic number increases

NOBLE GASES
Elements in this group have the following properties:

- Have eight valence electrons (exception: Helium (He), which has two valence electrons)

- Rarely react with other substances because they have a complete outer energy level

What about the two rows of elements that are
below the main periodic table?

These elements actually fit into the
table right after Group 2A. They are
often shown below the main table,
because the table would be too long
to fit on the page. These elements
are known as **LANTHANIDES**
and **ACTINIDES**.

Actinides, elements
89 to 103, are mostly
man-made elements that
don't exist in nature
(except for uranium
and plutonium).

Lanthanides, also called rare-earth metals,
comprise elements 57 to 71. They have properties that
are similar to lanthanide, which occurs at the beginning
of the row, and that's why they are called lanthanides.

PROPERTIES THAT DETERMINE TRENDS

When you look at the periodic table, you can see TRENDS,
or general directions of understanding, that explain the
properties of each element.

The properties to be aware of include:
**atomic radius, ionic radius, ionization energy, reactivity,
electronegativity**, and **valence electrons**.

It is important to understand how the protons in the nucleus affect the electrons in the outer shells. This is called **EFFECTIVE NUCLEAR CHARGE**.

Protons sit in an atom's nucleus and have positive charges. In an atom with more than one electron, that positive charge is distributed among the electrons, so that the full positive pull is not felt by any one electron.

> **EFFECTIVE NUCLEAR CHARGE**
> The net, or total, positive charge felt by an electron in an atom with multiple electrons.

In an atom with multiple levels of electrons, the higher-energy valence electrons are shielded from the full force of the positive pull from the protons by the electrons in the lower levels.

SHIELDING EFFECT is the balance between the positive attraction of protons on valence electrons and the repulsion forces from inner electrons.

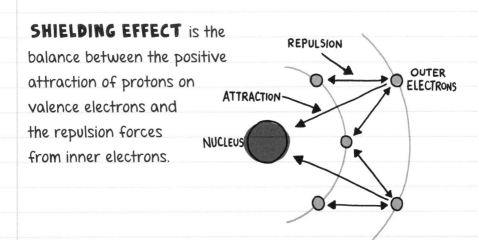

Atomic Radius

ATOMIC RADIUS is a measure of the size of the atoms. It is the typical distance from the center of the nucleus to the outermost electron.

JUST LIKE THE RADIUS IN MATH!

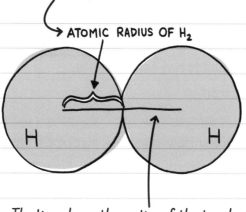

The measurement (in a straight line) from the center of the object to its edge.

ATOMIC RADIUS OF H_2

H   H

The line shows the radius of the two hydrogen atoms that make up the H_2 molecule.

As you move across a period from left to right, atomic radius decreases. This is because the effective nuclear charge increases as electrons are added into the energy level, which is the same distance from the nucleus.

Atomic radius increases from top to bottom in a group as the effective nuclear charge decreases, due to more electrons in more energy levels.

For example, magnesium has a larger atomic radius (is bigger) than chlorine. Magnesium is to the left of chlorine in the periodic table.

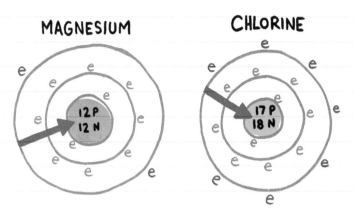

MAGNESIUM

CHLORINE

12 P
12 N

17 P
18 N

e = inner electrons, e = outer electrons, P = protons, N = neutrons. The arrows show the pull of the nuclei.

Ionic Radius

IONIC RADIUS is the measure of the distance between the center of the nuclei of two ions that barely touch.

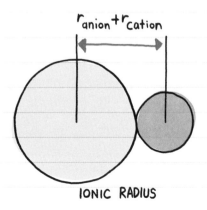

$r_{anion} + r_{cation}$

IONIC RADIUS

Ionic radius INCREASES for nonmetals moving across a period, because the effective nuclear charge (the force of attraction exerted by the protons) decreases as the number of electrons exceeds the number of protons. So, it gets bigger because the ion gains electrons.

> For a neutral atom, the atomic radius and ionic radius are equal. In an atom that has a charge, they are unequal.

The ionic radius decreases for metals moving left to right across a period, because they lose electrons and the effective nuclear charge increases.

So, the greater the nuclear charge, the more power being used to pull the electrons more tightly together, which makes the radius smaller.

Ionization Energy

IONIZATION ENERGY (IE) is the energy required to remove one or more electrons from a neutral atom in the gas phase. Not all atoms can give up electrons easily. In materials that hold electrons loosely, the electron that is farthest from the nucleus is relatively easy to pull off.

IE decreases from top to bottom in a group. As you move down a group, size increases as electrons are added in energy levels farther from the nucleus. The bigger the atoms, the less ionization energy that is needed to pull the electrons off, because the farther away electrons are from the nucleus, the weaker the attraction of the nucleus.

IE increases going left to right across the periodic table. As you move across a period, the effective nuclear charge increases as electrons are added at the same distance from the nucleus, making it harder to remove the electron.

Electronegativity

Atoms want to be in a stable state, and sometimes the only way to find that stability is to bond, or connect, with another atom. The connection between two atoms is called its **CHEMICAL BOND**. A chemical bond is the force that binds two or more atoms together by their electrons.

ELECTRONEGATIVITY is the tendency of an atom to
attract electrons in a chemical bond.

Electronegativity increases from bottom to top in a column.
Electronegativity increases from left to right across a group.

Noble gases do not have electronegativity values since they do not bond. F is most electronegative, Fr is least.

REACTIVITY TRENDS

REACTIVITY measures how likely an atom will react, or bond, with another atom. This depends on ionization energy (how difficult it is to get rid of that outer electron) and the number of valence electrons (how badly the atom needs to gain an extra electron).

Metals and nonmetals have opposite trends.

METALS

Reactivity increases as you move DOWN in a group. Reactivity decreases as you move ACROSS a period, from left to right. This is because metals react by losing electrons.

NONMETALS

Reactivity decreases as you move DOWN in a group. Reactivity increases as you move ACROSS a period, from left to right. Nonmetals react by gaining electrons.

Recap
Trends in the periodic table

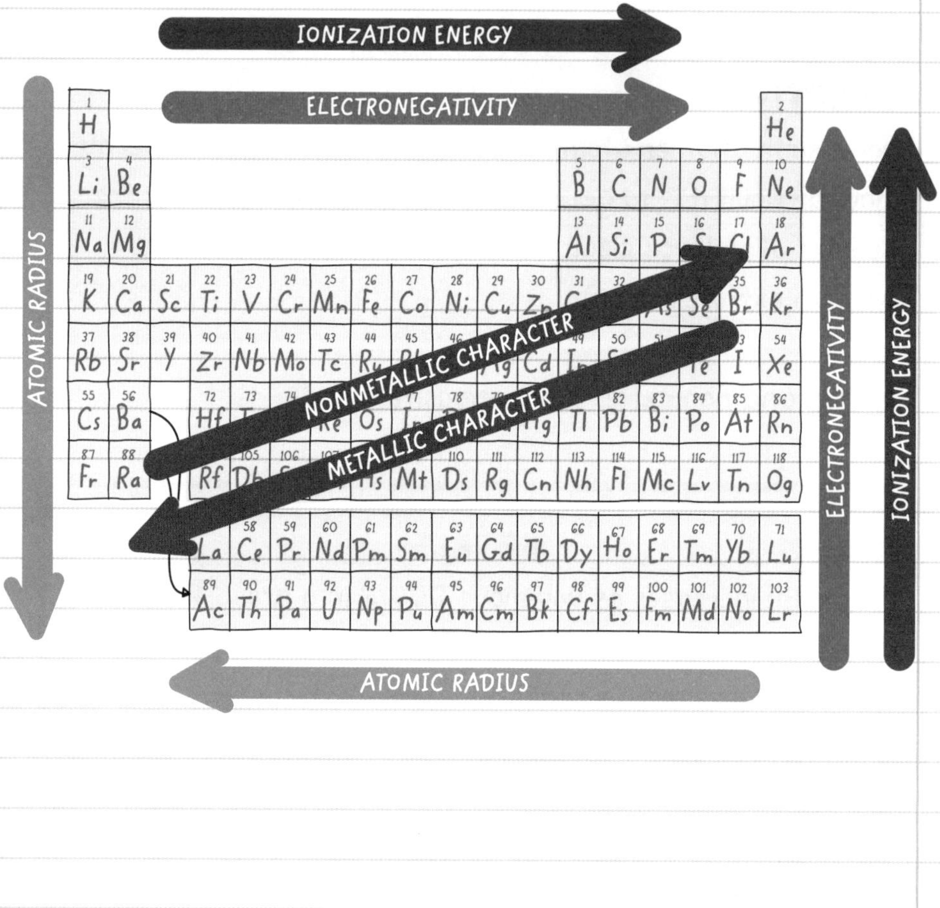

A periodic table showing trends. Arrows indicate:
- **IONIZATION ENERGY** — increases left to right across the table and bottom to top.
- **ELECTRONEGATIVITY** — increases left to right across the table and bottom to top.
- **ATOMIC RADIUS** — increases top to bottom and right to left.
- **NONMETALLIC CHARACTER** — increases diagonally toward the upper right.
- **METALLIC CHARACTER** — increases diagonally toward the lower left.

Periodic table entries:

1 H																	2 He
3 Li	4 Be											5 B	6 C	7 N	8 O	9 F	10 Ne
11 Na	12 Mg											13 Al	14 Si	15 P	16 S	17 Cl	18 Ar
19 K	20 Ca	21 Sc	22 Ti	23 V	24 Cr	25 Mn	26 Fe	27 Co	28 Ni	29 Cu	30 Zn	31 Ga	32 Ge	33 As	34 Se	35 Br	36 Kr
37 Rb	38 Sr	39 Y	40 Zr	41 Nb	42 Mo	43 Tc	44 Ru	45 Rh	46 Pd	47 Ag	48 Cd	49 In	50 Sn	51 Sb	52 Te	53 I	54 Xe
55 Cs	56 Ba		72 Hf	73 Ta	74 W	75 Re	76 Os	77 Ir	78 Pt	79 Au	80 Hg	81 Tl	82 Pb	83 Bi	84 Po	85 At	86 Rn
87 Fr	88 Ra		104 Rf	105 Db	106 Sg	107 Bh	108 Hs	109 Mt	110 Ds	111 Rg	112 Cn	113 Nh	114 Fl	115 Mc	116 Lv	117 Tn	118 Og

| 57 La | 58 Ce | 59 Pr | 60 Nd | 61 Pm | 62 Sm | 63 Eu | 64 Gd | 65 Tb | 66 Dy | 67 Ho | 68 Er | 69 Tm | 70 Yb | 71 Lu |
| 89 Ac | 90 Th | 91 Pa | 92 U | 93 Np | 94 Pu | 95 Am | 96 Cm | 97 Bk | 98 Cf | 99 Es | 100 Fm | 101 Md | 102 No | 103 Lr |

CHECK YOUR KNOWLEDGE

1. What law governs the periodic table?

2. What is a metalloid? Give a few examples of their properties.

3. Name five families of the periodic table.

4. What is the difference between atomic radius and ionic radius?

5. Explain the term *ionization* energy and describe its trends in the periodic table.

6. What is reactivity and what factors are important in its determination?

ANSWERS ➤ 169

CHECK YOUR ANSWERS

1. The periodic table is governed by periodic law.

2. Metalloids contain properties that are a mix of metal and nonmetal properties. They are solid at room temperature, can be dull or shiny, can be good conductors (whereas others are poor conductors of electricity and heat), and have physical properties that tend to be more like those of metals and chemical properties that tend to be more like those of nonmetals.

3. Five periodic table families are alkali metals, alkaline-earth metals, transition metals, halogens, and noble gases.

4. Atomic radius is the measure of the size of the atoms. The typical distance is measured from the center of the nucleus to the outermost electron. Ionic radius is the measure of half of the distance between the nuclei of two ions.

5. Ionization energy (IE) is the energy required to remove one or more electrons from a neutral atom in the gas phase. IE decreases from top to bottom in a group and increases going from left to right across the periodic table.

6. Reactivity measures the likelihood of an atom to react, or bond, with another atom. Reactivity is dependent on ionization energy and the number of valence electrons that an element possesses.

Chapter 13

ELECTRONS

ENERGY LEVELS

The first scientist to come up with a plan on the structure of the atom was NIELS BOHR.

Bohr wanted to know where the electrons were located in the atom. He proposed the idea that electrons zoomed around the nucleus like the planets zoom around the sun, in an **ORBIT**.

> **ORBIT**
> The curved path that an object takes around another object.

Bohr called these orbits **ENERGY LEVELS**.

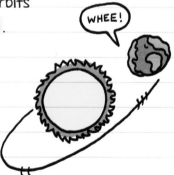

WHEE!

Bohr's rules for energy levels:

● **Each energy level has a specific size and energy**. The energy of the level is related to its size: the smaller the level, the lower the energy.

● **Each energy level is a fixed distance from the nucleus**. The levels are numbered, starting from the nucleus and moving out.

Bohr thought that the only way electrons could gain or lose energy was to move from one energy level to another.

Bohr's model of the element calcium (Ca):

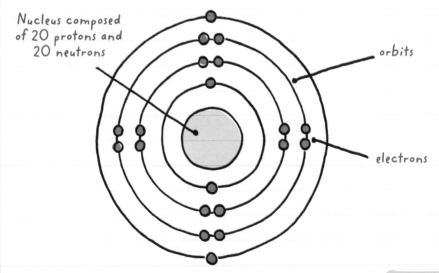

Nucleus composed of 20 protons and 20 neutrons

orbits

electrons

Electrons in the outermost energy level are called
VALENCE ELECTRONS.

- When an electron moves from a higher energy level
  (farther away from the nucleus) to a lower level (closer
  to the nucleus), it releases energy, emitting a photon in
  the process.

Scientists later realized that Bohr's model was incorrect. The
model said that energy levels were specific distances from
the nucleus, but that was proven to be incorrect. However,
Bohr was the first to suggest a structure for how the
electrons occupy the atom.

PARTICLE OR WAVE?

Scientists were still confused about how electrons behaved.
Did they act like waves? Or were they quantum packages,
like particles? LOUIS DE BROGLIE said they were both.
de Broglie proved that waves can behave like particles
and particles can behave like waves.

The scientist WERNER HEISENBERG said that we cannot
know exactly where an electron is located when it behaves
like a wave. That is because waves extend into space,
which means they go on and on.

Heisenberg developed the HEISENBERG UNCERTAINTY PRINCIPLE, which stated that it is impossible to know, simultaneously and with certainty, both the momentum and the position of a particle.

This means that the structured orbits, or energy level paths, that Bohr came up with were wrong. The orbits/energy levels were not well-defined paths, but more like an area of space where the electron might be located.

Austrian physicist ERWIN SCHRÖDINGER pulled all of these theories together into one equation known as the Schrödinger equation. This equation is the basis for **QUANTUM MECHANICS**, the science that explains the interactions of atoms and subatomic particles such as electrons, protons, and neutrons.

Important things to know about Schrödinger's equation:

- It uses both wave behavior and particle behavior in the same equation.

- The probability of finding an electron in a certain place is proportional to the square of the wave function.

- The most likely place to find a photon is where the intensity of the light is the greatest.

- The formula cannot tell you where the electron is exactly, but it gives you the probability of where it can be found at any given time.

- The energy states and wave functions are described by a set of quantum numbers.

Recap

Electrons move constantly within an atom.

You can never know exactly where electrons are.

Electrons will always head for the lowest energy level first and fill up the shells from the nucleus outward.

Electrons in the outermost energy levels are called valence electrons.

SUMMATION? IN CHEMISTRY, IT'S ALL ABOUT THE ELECTRON!

CHECK YOUR KNOWLEDGE

1. What happens when an electron moves from a higher energy level to a lower one?

2. Who was the first scientist to propose that an electron could act both like a wave and a particle?

3. What does the Heisenberg Uncertainty Principle state?

4. Who founded quantum mechanics?

5. Why was Schrödinger's equation so revolutionary?

ANSWERS

1. When an electron moves from a higher energy level to a lower one, it loses energy by emitting a photon. Bohr was the first scientist to make this suggestion, which allowed for every type of observation to be accounted for.

2. de Broglie was the first scientist to propose that an electron could act both like a wave and a particle.

3. The Heisenberg Uncertainty Principle states that it is impossible to know, simultaneously and with certainty, both the momentum and the position of a particle.

4. Schrödinger, Heisenberg, and Max Planck have been considered the founders of quantum mechanics.

5. Schrödinger's equation was revolutionary because it uses both wave behavior and particle behavior in the same equation.

Unit 5

Bonding and VSEPR Theory

Chapter 14

BONDING

CHEMICAL BONDS

When two or more atoms combine, they form a chemical **BOND**, the force that holds the atoms together. Atoms form chemical bonds to complete their outer energy levels and become more stable. Only the electrons in the outer shell (valence electrons) form chemical bonds. Atoms form bonds according to the octet rule.

OCTET MEANS A GROUP OF EIGHT.

Octet Rule: Elements combine in such a way that each atom has a complete outer energy level, which is eight for many elements. For this to happen, atoms give up or take electrons from each other to balance out their electron count.

The valence number of most atoms can be determined by their location on the periodic table. The number of valence electrons is the same as the group number.

For example:

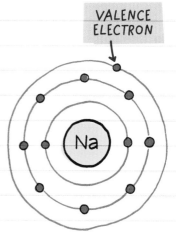

Sodium (Na) is in the first group in the periodic table and has one valence electron. It looks like this:

Chlorine (Cl) is in the seventh group and has seven valence electrons. It looks like this:

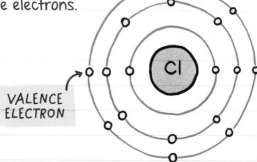

Exceptions: Transition metals usually have either two or three valence electrons, although some can have as many as five or six.

Atoms bond to complete their outer energy level and become more stable. Noble gases are the most stable elements. They already have full energy levels (two electrons for helium (He) and eight electrons each for neon (Ne), argon (Ar), krypton (Kr), xenon (Xe), and radon (Rn)). All other elements want to be stable like them. The type of bond that atoms form determines how stable they will become.

The three main types of bonds are:

IONIC: One atom donates electron(s), the other accepts the electrons, and a bond is formed by attraction between the newly formed ions. This occurs between metal and nonmetal ions.

COVALENT: Two atoms share electrons between them. This occurs between two nonmetals.

METALLIC: Atoms are connected via a "sea of electrons." This only occurs between metals.

IONIC BONDS

Ionic bonds occur when two atoms are connected to each other by **ELECTROSTATIC ATTRACTION**, when two oppositely charged objects are attracted to each other.

Ionic bonds happen between a metal cation and a nonmetal anion.

A **cation** is a positively charged ion.

An **anion** is a negatively charged ion.

ELECTROSTATIC ATTRACTION
Occurs when oppositely charged ions are attracted to one another.

Metals vs Nonmetals

Metals have fewer valence electrons than nonmetals and tend to lose them to complete their octet. The energy required to remove an electron from a neutral atom is called its IONIZATION ENERGY.

Ionization energy (IE) + metal atom →
                        metal cation (+) + electron (e^-)

When you add ionization energy to a metal ion, the metal will lose an electron and become a metal cation.

Nonmetals have more valence electrons and tend to gain more to complete their octet. The energy given off by an atom when it gains electrons is called its **ELECTRON AFFINITY**.

Nonmetal atom + electron (e⁻) →

         nonmetal anion (–) + energy (electron affinity)

A nonmetal atom will add an electron to fill its valence shell, making it a nonmetal anion plus energy.

FOR EXAMPLE: Sodium (Na) and chlorine (Cl) bond to make table salt (NaCl).

Sodium has one valence electron (red electron) that it donates to chlorine.

Sodium ion is 1+ (it donated one electron).

Chlorine ion is –1 (it gained the extra electron from sodium).

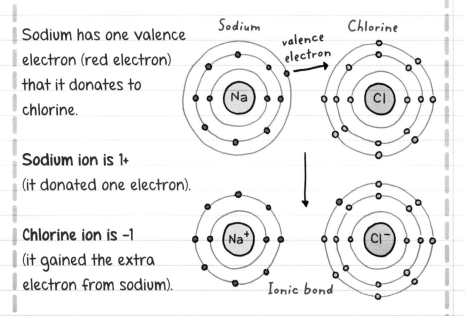

When the two ions bond, they form the ionically bonded, stable compound **NaCl**. The red electron from the sodium is donated to the outer shell of the chlorine atom.

SIMPLE AND POLYATOMIC IONS

A **SIMPLE ION** is formed from a single ion. Examples of simple ions are those atoms in groups 1 and 2 of the periodic table, which lose their electrons easily. They do this because it is easy to lose one or two electrons to gain a full valence shell.

Examples of simple ions:

hydrogen (H^+), lithium (Li^+), sodium (Na^+), potassium (K^+),

beryllium (Be^{2+}), magnesium (Mg^{2+}), and calcium (Ca^{2+})

A **POLYATOMIC ION** is formed when two or more atoms join together.

Examples of polyatomic ions:

NH_4^+: Ammonium ion, comprised of one atom of nitrogen (N) and four atoms of hydrogen (H)

OH^-: Hydroxide ion, comprised of one atom of oxygen (O) and one atom of hydrogen (H)

NH_4^+ combines with OH^- to make NH_4OH (ammonium hydroxide)

Ammonium hydroxide is a neutral compound that is ionically bonded.

> **Note about stability:** Atoms that gain or lose electrons to create a full outer energy level are more stable than a neutral atom.

FOR EXAMPLE: Explain how calcium and oxygen bond to form a compound of calcium oxide (CaO).

The arrows show that the two electrons from calcium are donated to the oxygen atom, so that the oxygen and the calcium have full octets.

$$Ca + \ddot{O}: \rightarrow Ca^{2+} :\ddot{\ddot{O}}:^{2-}$$

Step 1: Check the periodic table to determine the number of valence electrons.

Ca is in group 2. It has two valence electrons (shown by the black dots around each chemical symbol in the drawing).

O is in group 4: It has six valence electrons.

Step 2: Determine who will donate and who will accept the electrons.

If an element has less than three electrons in its outer shell, it will donate—or give away—these electrons. If the element has more than five electrons, it will accept or add new electrons.

Ca will give up its electrons to get a full octet: Ca^{2+}.

The 2+ shows that calcium has given up two of its electrons. Each electron is -1, so if they give up two electrons their charge will become -2.

O will accept electrons to get a full octet: O^{2-}.

The 2- means that oxygen has accepted two electrons from calcium and has gained a -2 charge.

The compound that calcium and oxygen will form is CaO. There are no numbers in the final compound, because +2 and -2 cancel each other out.

1. Check the periodic table to determine the number of valence electrons.

   Na is in group 1, so it has one valence electron.

   OH is an ion that accepts an electron, so its charge is now −1.

2. Determine who will donate and who will accept the electrons.

   Na will give up its electron to get a full octet of Na+ (when the superscript is 1, you just show the sign and not 1+ or 1−).

   Hydroxide accepts one electron to result in a charge of OH−.

3. The compound that they will form is NaOH.

The total positive charge of the cations will be equal to the total negative charge of the anions that are being accepted by the anion. So, the overall charge on an ionic compound is zero.

Ionic compounds:

- Have electrostatic attractions that are quite strong and difficult to break.

- Have high melting and boiling points.

- Are hard and brittle.

- Are salts, which means that they are made from a metal and a nonmetal. Exceptions include oxides (metal + oxygen) and hydroxides (metal + hydrogen).

Salts are neutral compounds that have high melting and boiling points. When dissolved in water, they can conduct electricity, because in a solution they dissociate into ions.

Ionic compounds are arranged in a **CRYSTAL LATTICE**, a three-dimensional structure that is created when a salt compound forms.

Nonmetal anions are larger in size than metal cations. Therefore, the cations fit into the spaces between the anions as they line up.

A crystal lattice may be drawn
like this:

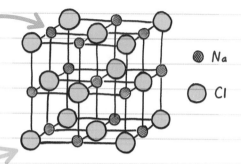

Na is the cation

Cl is the anion

Na

Cl

Ionic bonds form due to the large difference in
electronegativity among the ions.

ELECTRONEGATIVITY
is **not** the same as electron affinity:

Electron affinity is the energy change when
an electron is accepted by a neutral atom.

Electronegativity is the ability of an atom to
attract itself to the electrons in a chemical bond.

The difference in electronegativity is easy to see when two
elements from opposite sides of the periodic chart bond.

For example, fluorine (F) is from group 7 and it bonds with
lithium (Li) from group 1. Lithium forms a bond by donating
an electron. Fluorine forms a bond by accepting an electron.

Electronegativity increases across the period, from left to right. Lithium is not as electronegative as fluorine (which is very electronegative), and they make a strong ionic bond.

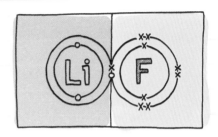

Ionic bonds will form so that their total charge is neutral, even if that indicates more than one of the same element is required.

FOR EXAMPLE: Suppose magnesium (Mg) wants to bond with chlorine (Cl).

Mg is in group 2, so it wants to give up two electrons to complete its octet. This means that the Mg ion has a charge of Mg^{+2}.

Cl is in group 7, so it wants to accept one electron to complete its octet.

The Cl ion has a charge of Cl^-.

So, if Mg^{2+} combines with Cl^-, it will still have an overall charge of 1+ because magnesium wants to give up two electrons but chlorine can only take one.

BUT, if you had two Cl ions, they would each accept one electron.

Now, it looks like this:

$Mg^{2+} + 2\ Cl^- \rightarrow MgCl_2$ (a stable compound)

Ionic compounds conduct electricity when they are dissolved in water.

Water causes the ionic compound to break up into ions again. This is called **DISSOCIATION**. Once the cations and anions are free to float around, they can conduct electricity.

COVALENT BONDS

Covalent bonds form when two or more atoms want to share electrons. The sharing must allow for all atoms to obtain a full octet (complete their outer energy level).

Covalent bonding occurs mostly between nonmetals that are close to each other on the periodic table. This is because elements will have similar electronegativity. In other words, they both want to gain electrons.

For example, carbon (C) has four valence electrons. To form an ionic bond, it would have to gain or lose four electrons (that's a lot). Not only would that need to occur, but it would also have to find another element that wanted to gain or lose four electrons. This is not very likely. Carbon solves this problem by sharing its electrons with another atom.

PROPERTIES OF COVALENT BONDS

- Low melting and boiling points (except for network covalent bonds).
- Softer than ionic bonds.
- Don't conduct electricity.
- Don't dissolve well in water.
- More flammable than ionic compounds.

The easiest way to see how covalent bonds work is to look at a LEWIS DOT DIAGRAM.

The Lewis dot diagram is named for GILBERT N. LEWIS, an American physical chemist, who in 1916 was the first to draw an actual image of a compound showing the bonding pair of electrons and the lone (nonbonded) pair of electrons for each element.

A Lewis dot diagram uses a dot "•" as the symbol for each valence electron. Because most atoms try to have eight (the octet rule), the valence electrons are shown as pairs on each side of the element symbol.

This is the Lewis dot diagram for neon (Ne). It has eight valence electrons around it, because it is a noble gas with eight electrons in its outer energy level.

valence electrons

:Ne:

This is a Lewis dot diagram for phosphorous (P). It has five valence electrons.

This is a Lewis dot diagram for chlorine (Cl), in group 7. It has seven valence electrons.

When phosphorous and chlorine combine, they form a covalent bond. They *share* three electrons.

$$:\overset{\cdot}{\underset{\cdot\cdot}{Cl}}\cdot \quad \cdot\overset{\cdot\cdot}{P}\quad \cdot\overset{\cdot\cdot}{\underset{\cdot\cdot}{Cl}}: \quad \longrightarrow \quad :\overset{\cdot\cdot}{\underset{\cdot\cdot}{Cl}}:\overset{\cdot\cdot}{P}:\overset{\cdot\cdot}{\underset{\cdot\cdot}{Cl}}:$$

$$:\overset{\cdot}{\underset{\cdot\cdot}{Cl}}:$$

Chlorine's valence electrons are in red.

Phosphorous's valence electrons are in blue.

Phosphorous has only five electrons in its valence shell, so it needs to bond with three atoms of chlorine that each provide one atom for the bonding pair.

The sharing of electrons occurs where you can see both red and blue electrons on one side. These are called **BONDING PAIRS**.

The pairs that are not bonded are called **LONE PAIRS**.

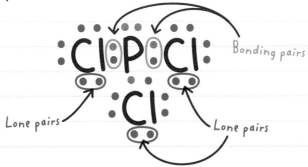

Bonding pairs

Lone pairs

Lone pairs

195

Diatomic Molecules

Sometimes, atoms will form covalent bonds with themselves to become more stable. These are called **DIATOMIC MOLECULES**.

Room temperature is used to compare diatomic molecules, because that is the most common condition under which they are used.

The seven diatomic molecules at room temperature are:

Nitrogen	N_2	gas
Oxygen	O_2	gas
Fluorine	F_2	gas
Iodine	I_2	solid
Bromine	Br_2	liquid
Hydrogen	H_2	gas
Chlorine	Cl_2	gas

You can indicate bonding by including two dots or a single horizontal line between the two atoms.

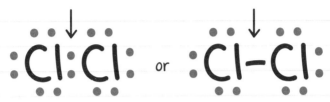

DOUBLE AND TRIPLE COVALENT BONDS

Some atoms will form multiple covalent bonds to complete their outer energy levels, thus becoming more stable.

A **DOUBLE BOND** occurs when two atoms share four electrons.

A **TRIPLE BOND** occurs when two atoms share six electrons.

Oxygen (O_2) forms a diatomic molecule with a double bond.

Oxygen has six valence electrons. When it shares two electrons with another oxygen atom, it achieves an octet. That bond can be shown in different ways.

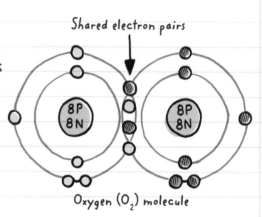

Shared electron pairs

Oxygen (O_2) molecule

:Ö:Ö: :Ö=Ö:

In the models above, the shared electron pairs are shown as dots between the two oxygen atoms or with the two lines, which indicate a double bond that is equal to two pairs of shared electrons.

A triple bond is formed in the compound carbon dioxide (CO_2).

Carbon has four valence electrons.

CARBON DIOXIDE

Oxygen has six valence electrons.

Oxygen   Carbon   Oxygen

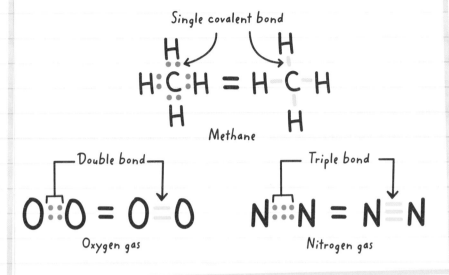

WAYS TO INDICATE COVALENT BONDS:

Single covalent bond

H:C:H = H C H

Methane

Double bond

O::O = O O

Oxygen gas

Triple bond

N:::N = N N

Nitrogen gas

EXCEPTIONS TO THE OCTET RULE

Most atoms bond according to the octet rule, but there are some exceptions:

Molecules in which one or more of the atoms have fewer than eight electrons

applies to hydrogen and helium only

THE DUET RULE For helium and hydrogen, a full valence shell consists of only two electrons. They will bond with themselves to form diatomic molecules with only two atoms.

$$H\cdot + H\cdot \rightarrow H\!:\!H$$

Hydrogen bonds with itself to have two electrons in its valence shell.

Helium will do the same, but will only share two electrons and have one electron in its outer shell.

Some Group 3 Elements:

Boron (B) has three valence electrons. It wants to find an element that has five electrons, but boron is a small atom. Five extra electrons don't fit easily around its nucleus, so it settles for a covalent bond with its three valence electrons.

Boron (B) combines with hydrogen (H) in the following way to form BH_3:

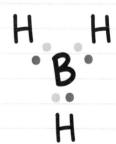

CHECK YOUR KNOWLEDGE

1. What is the octet rule? Why is it important?

2. What are the three main types of chemical bonds?

3. Between what two types of atoms are ionic bonds found? What about covalent bonds?

4. What is the difference between ionic and covalent bonds?

5. Why are elements that bond covalently found close to each other on the periodic table?

6. Name three properties of covalent compounds.

7. What is the difference between bonding pairs and lone pairs?

8. Define a diatomic molecule and give an example.

9. How many covalent bonds are used in the formation of N_2? Draw the Lewis dot diagram for N_2.

10. Name two elements whose outer energy levels are complete with two electrons.

ANSWERS

CHECK YOUR ANSWERS

1. The octet rule states that elements want to combine in such a way that each atom has eight electrons in their valence shells. It is the basic guide for the way in which atoms combine.

2. The three main types of chemical bonds are ionic, covalent, and metallic.

3. Ionic bonds occur between a metal and a nonmetal. Covalent bonds usually occur between two nonmetal atoms.

4. Ionic bonds form when atoms donate or accept electrons. Covalent bonds form when atoms share their electron-bonded pair.

5. Elements that are close to each other on the periodic table have similar electronegativities. In other words, they both want to gain electrons.

6. They have low melting and boiling points, are softer than ionic bonds, don't conduct electricity because they don't have any free electrons, don't dissolve well in water, and are more flammable than ionic compounds.

7. Bonding pairs are shared between two atoms. Lone pairs are electrons for only one atom.

8. A diatomic molecule occurs when atoms form covalent bonds with themselves to become more stable. Examples are H_2, Cl_2, N_2, etc.

9. A covalent triple bond is used in the formation of N_2.

$$:\dot{N}\cdot \ + \ \cdot\dot{N}: \ \longrightarrow \ :N:::N:$$

$$(:N\equiv N:)$$

10. Hydrogen (H) and helium (He) are examples of two elements whose outer energy levels are complete with two electrons.

Chapter 15

VALENCE SHELL ELECTRON PAIR REPULSION (VSEPR) THEORY

REPRESENTING MOLECULES

Lewis dot diagrams work well to show the bonding of electrons between atoms, but they are two-dimensional (2-D) and do not show the arrangement of atoms in a three-dimensional (3-D) space. That 3-D arrangement illustrates the **MOLECULAR GEOMETRY** of the molecule.

Molecular geometry is the 3-D arrangement of atoms within a molecule.

VALENCE SHELL ELECTRON PAIR REPULSION

THEORY (VSEPR) allows scientists to predict the 3-D shape of a molecule that is centered around a central atom. VSEPR shows a molecule's appearance in three dimensions. Electrons don't like to be next to each other; they repel, because they are all negative. But there are several electrons, so they have to find the positions with the smallest repulsion.

VSEPR uses the following rules:

- Electron pairs in the valence shell of an atom will repel or move away from each other.

- Nonbonded electron pairs are found closer to the atom and exhibit more repulsion than bonded pairs.

VSEPR molecules have five basic shapes:

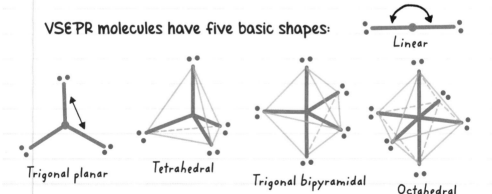

Trigonal planar

Tetrahedral

Trigonal bipyramidal

Octahedral

Linear

Double or triple covalent bonds are treated just like single bonds in a VSEPR diagram: They are represented with a single bar.

How the Structures Are Formed

Atoms arrange themselves to be as far away from each other as possible. For example, beryllium fluoride (BeF_2) has two bonds. The fluorine (F) atoms want to be as far away from each other as possible (otherwise, their electrons will repel), so they occupy positions at a 180-degree angle to make a linear (straight) structure. Imagine having to walk two dogs who didn't like each other. They would want to be as far away from each other as possible.

BF_3 has three bonds, so being linear doesn't work. Think of geometry class. If the F atoms need to arrange themselves around a boron (B) atom to maximize the space between them, they will occupy positions to create 120-degree angles between them.

NOW, THIS IS JUST RIDICULOUS!

As you add more bonds, the electrons repel each other to maximize the distance between them.

POLAR VS NONPOLAR BONDS

Covalent bonds are classified as being either **polar** or nonpolar. **POLARITY**, a physical property of the compound, is important because it determines other physical properties of the compound, such as boiling point, melting point, solubility, and intermolecular interactions.

Atoms using **NONPOLAR BONDS** equally share the electrons between them, due to the similar electronegativity values of the atoms in the molecule.

POLAR BONDS have unequal sharing of electrons between atoms, due to the different electronegativity values of the atoms in the molecule.

All ionic bonds are polar bonds.

In a polar covalent bond, the electrons are shared, but they can be found more on one side. It's like sharing a blanket where you have two-thirds of it and the other person has one-third.

In a polar covalent bond, the side that is closer to the bonded pair of electrons is slightly more negative. This means that the other side of the bond is slightly more positive. This small difference in charge is called a **DIPOLE**.

Because the charges are partial (less than 1), they are written as δ+ and δ-.

> δ (read as delta) means slightly
>
> δ+ means slightly positive
>
> δ- means slightly negative

$$\overset{\delta+}{} \quad \overset{\delta-}{}$$
$$H-Cl$$

The notation shows that the H side is slightly more positive and the Cl side slightly negative, because hydrogen tends to give up an electron and chlorine tends to gain one.

How can you tell whether the sharing is equal?

Electronegativity values can be used to classify a bond as polar covalent, nonpolar covalent, or ionic. Below is a list of the electronegativity values for each element. You can use the values to compare element electronegativities.

H 2.1																	He
Li 1.0	Be 1.6											B 2.0	C 2.5	N 3.0	O 3.5	F 4.0	Ne
Na 0.9	Mg 1.2											Al 1.5	Si 1.8	P 2.1	S 2.5	Cl 3.00	Ar
K 0.2	Ca 1.0	Sc 1.3	Ti 1.5	V 1.6	Cr 1.66	Mn 1.5	Fe 1.8	Co 1.8	Ni 1.8	Cu 1.9	Zn 1.6	Ga 1.8	Ge 1.8	As 2.0	Se 2.4	Br 2.8	Kr 3.0
Rb 0.2	Sr 1.0	Y 1.2	Zr 1.4	Nb 1.6	Mo 1.8	Tc 1.9	Ru 2.2	Rh 2.2	Pd 2.2	Ag 1.9	Cd 1.7	In 1.7	Sn 1.8	Sb 1.9	Te 2.1	I 2.5	Xe 2.5
Cs 0.9	Ba 0.9	La 1.1	Hf 1.3	Ta 1.5	W 1.7	Re 1.9	Os 2.2	Ir 2.2	Pt 2.2	Au 2.4	Hg 1.9	Tl 1.8	Pb 1.8	Bi 1.8	Po 2.0	At 2.2	Rn 2.4
Fr 0.7	Ra 0.7	Ac 1.1	Rf	Db	Sg	Bh	Hs	Mt	Uun	Uuu	Uub						

Lanthanides	Ce 1.1	Pr 1.1	Nd 1.1	Pm 1.1	Sm 1.1	Eu 1.1	Gd 1.1	Tb 1.1	Dy 1.1	Ho 1.1	Er 1.1	Tm 1.1	Yb 1.1	Lu 1.2
Actinides	Th 1.3	Pa 1.5	U 1.7	Np 1.3	Pu 1.3	Am 1.3	Cm 1.3	Bk 1.3	Cr 1.3	Es 1.3	Fm 1.3	Md 1.3	No 1.3	Lr 1.8

Electronegativity data is not available for the elements not shown.

This drawing of hydrogen chloride (HCl) shows the **DIPOLE MOMENT** of the molecule, which is indicated by an arrow with a line across one end. The vertical bar at the left end of the arrow shows the element that is donating the electron. The arrowhead end shows the direction in which the electrons are moving, toward the element that is accepting the electron. Because no arrow is heading in the opposite direction, HCl is considered to be a polar molecule.

$\delta+$ $\delta-$

H–C̈l̈:

⊢→

The arrow also points to the more electronegative atom, indicating where the electrons are most likely to be found.

Diatomic molecules such as O_2, H_2, and N_2 have no difference in electronegativity values because the electronegativity of each atom is the same. These molecules are nonpolar, but the atoms do not need to be the same for the bond to be labeled nonpolar.

Carbon's electronegativity is 2.5 and hydrogen's value is 2.1.

Nonpolar covalent bonds form between atoms with an electronegativity difference of between 0 and 0.4.

2.5 – 2.1 = 0.4

0.4 rounds down to zero.
Therefore, a bond between
carbon and hydrogen is
nonpolar.

> Polar covalent bonds form
> between atoms with
> an electronegativity difference
> of between 0.5 and 1.7.

MOLECULAR POLARITY
IN BONDS

Molecular polarity depends on the shape of the molecule and
how the electron pairs occupy space.

> Bonds are polar if the atoms have an electronegativity
> difference greater than 0.5. The entire molecular
> is polar if the shape is asymmetric.

For example, if you write CH_4 with the
structural formula, it looks like this,
which appears to be linear. But if
you apply VSEPR, it looks more like a
tetrahedron, showing electron pairs
that are far apart from one another
in a 3-D model.

$$H-\overset{\displaystyle H}{\underset{\displaystyle H}{C}}-H$$

Lewis dot structure

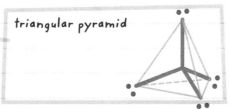

triangular pyramid

In the model, the straight bonds are in a 2-D plane, The dotted line represents the atom away from you, and the bold line represents the H closest to you.

straight bonds

dotted line

H
|
H—C ····ıH
|
H

bold line

VSEPR structure

Because of its geometry, the molecule is nonpolar overall.

Nonpolar molecules include:

SNAP
Symmetrical molecules are **N**onpolar and **A**symmetric molecules are **P**olar.

☐ CO_2

☐ Any of the noble gases

☐ Any diatomic molecules, such as H_2 and Cl_2

☐ Many carbon compounds, such as CCl_4, CH_4, and C_6H_6

Can a molecule be nonpolar but the bonds are polar at the same time?

YES

It is possible for the individual bonds in a molecule to be polar while the overall molecule is nonpolar. That means some of the bonds within the molecule have slight dipoles, but overall, the molecule itself distributes the dipoles equally in space.

For example, in carbon dioxide (CO_2), carbon forms a double bond with each oxygen. But each oxygen has six lone electrons. These are very electronegative and pull the electrons in the covalent bond toward them, causing a dipole to form.

This does not mean that it's a polar molecule.

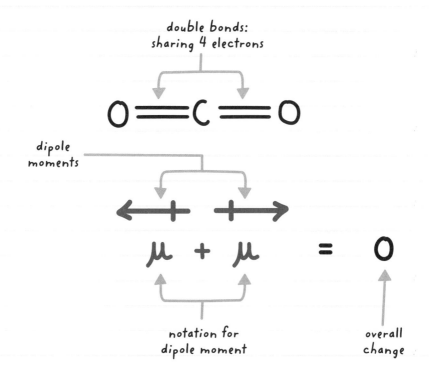

double bonds:
sharing 4 electrons

dipole
moments

notation for
dipole moment

overall
change

The geometric shape, which is linear, cancels out the dipole moment, making the overall charge 0. Therefore, it is a nonpolar molecule.

Characteristics of ionic, polar, and nonpolar bonds.

Comparison of Ionic, Polar, and Nonpolar Bonding

IONIC	COVALENT	
Ions (metal + nonmetal)	Polar (two different nonmetals)	Nonpolar (two identical nonmetals)
Complete transfer of electrons	Unequal sharing of electrons	Equal sharing of electrons
Full ionic charges	Partial ionic charges	No charges
Na+Cl-	H ⟶ Cl	H – H

CHECK YOUR KNOWLEDGE

1. What is molecular geometry and why is it so important in chemistry?

2. How do nonbonded pairs behave differently from bonded pairs of electrons?

3. What are the five basic VSEPR arrangements?

4. Draw the Lewis dot diagram and VSEPR diagram of CH_4.

5. What is the difference between a polar and a nonpolar bond?

6. Define a dipole. What symbols are used to show that a dipole is present?

7. How does electronegativity difference determine bond polarity?

ANSWERS

CHECK YOUR ANSWERS

1. Molecular geometry is the three-dimensional arrangement of atoms within a molecule. It helps to determine the structure of a molecule, which determines its properties.

2. Nonbonded electron pairs are found closer to the atom and exhibit more repulsion than bonded pairs.

3. The five basic VSEPR arrangements are linear, trigonal planar, tetrahedral, trigonal bipyramidal, and octahedral.

4.

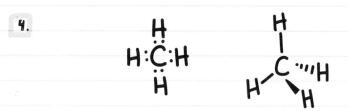

5. Nonpolar bonds have an equal sharing of the electrons between the atoms. Polar bonds have an unequal sharing of electrons between atoms.

6. A dipole occurs when the side that has elements with more electronegativity is slightly more negative. That means the other side of the bond is slightly more positive. This small difference in charge is called a dipole. Because the charges are less than 1, they are written as delta plus ($\delta+$) and delta minus ($\delta-$).

7. Polar covalent bonds form between atoms with an electronegativity difference of between 0.5 and 1.7. Nonpolar bonds do not have a large difference in electronegativity.

Chapter 16

METALLIC BONDS AND INTRAMOLECULAR FORCES

METALLIC BONDS

Metallic bonds are formed when two metal atoms share the electrons between them. Metallic bonds are different from covalent bonds, because the bonding electrons are **DELOCALIZED**, which means that they are free to move around. Metallic bonds are said to have a sea of mobile electrons or an **ELECTRON SEA**.

ELECTRON SEA
The body of delocalized, or free-floating, electrons that surround cations (positive metal ions in metallic bonds).

The red circles represent the nucleus of each metal atom. The blue dots represent the electrons, which float freely around the nuclei.

Metallic bonds are found between metals or in metal alloys, a mixture of metals. Examples are:

Gold bars

Copper wire

Aluminum foil

Steel girders

Properties of Metallic Bonds

Metals exhibit properties based on the bonds that they contain. Metals:

- are good conductors for both electricity and heat; because their electrons can move about, they easily carry a charge.

- have high melting points and boiling points; metallic bonds are strong and require a lot of energy to break them.

- have high density.

- are malleable and ductile.

MALLEABLE
Able to be pressed or hammered into sheets.

DUCTILE
Able to be stretched into a thin wire.

The strength of a metallic bond depends on the number of electrons that are free to move about the metal and the size and charge of the cation (metal).

	TYPE OF BOND		
	COVALENT	METALLIC	IONIC
DEFINITION	Shared pair of electrons	Electron sea	Transfer of electrons in the valence shell
OCCURRENCE	Between two nonmetals	Between two metals	Between a metal and a nonmetal
MELTING/BOILING POINTS	Low	High	High
HARDNESS	Not very hard, except for diamond, silicon, and carbon	Hard	Hard
ELECTRICAL CONDUCTIVITY	None	High	Only when in liquids or dissolved

Some compounds that contain POLYATOMIC IONS may have more than one type of bonding. For example, calcium carbonate ($CaCO_3$), found in bones and seashells, has covalent bonds holding the CO_3^{-2} ion together in the polyatomic ion that is known as carbonate. The Ca^{+2} ions are attracted to the negative CO_3^{-2} ions, creating an ionic bond.

Other compounds that contain both bonds include $MgSO_4$, $NaHCO_3$, and $NaOH$.

INTERMOLECULAR FORCES

Two types of forces or attractions describe how molecules and atoms interact.

INTRAMOLECULAR FORCES hold the molecule or compound together. These are covalent, ionic, and metallic bonds, which determine many chemical properties of the substance.

INTERMOLECULAR FORCES, the forces between the molecules, influence their physical properties, such as boiling point or melting point.

Intra means <u>inside or within</u> molecules and refers to the forces that interact within a single molecule.

Inter means <u>outside or external</u> to the molecules, such as two molecules bonding together.

Intermolecular forces from weakest to strongest:

- London dispersion
- Dipole-dipole interactions
- Hydrogen bonding

> Weaker intermolecular forces are also called
> VAN DER WAALS FORCES, after the Dutch physicist
> JOHANNES VAN DER WAALS, who discovered them.

London Dispersion Forces

LONDON DISPERSION FORCES (LDFs) are extremely weak attractive forces that are created by the movement of electrons, which attract to the positive nucleus of another atom. This leads to temporary dipoles that loosely "stick" atoms together.

- London forces are temporary. The constant motion of electrons within the atom allows it to form a temporary dipole.

- London dispersion forces are present in both polar AND nonpolar molecules.

- More electrons mean stronger LDFs.

London dispersion forces are named for the physicist FRITZ LONDON, who discovered them in 1930.

Dipole-Dipole Interactions

DIPOLE FORCES are the attraction forces that occur between two polar molecules. These polar molecules have dipole forces, because the electrons are pulled to the more electronegative end of the covalent bond, creating a **DIPOLE MOMENT**. Positive attracts negative, and negative attracts positive.

> **DIPOLE MOMENT**
> When electrical charges with opposite signs are separated by a distance, they form an electric dipole. The dipole moment measures the size of the dipole.

> A dipole force is the attraction between the positive end of one polar molecule and the negative end of another polar molecule.

HCl (hydrochloric acid) has a dipole moment that looks like this:

$$^{+\delta} \text{H} —\text{Cl}\ ^{-\delta}$$

The strong electronegativity of chlorine pulls the electrons away from the hydrogen. Either end of this polar molecule would be attracted to water (H_2O), which is also a polar molecule.

$$^{+\delta} \text{H} —\text{Cl}\ ^{-\delta}$$

$$\text{H}^{\delta+} \quad \mu \quad \text{H}^{\delta+}$$
$$\text{O}$$
$$\delta^{2-}$$

223

The two hydrogen-positive dipoles will be attracted to the negative dipole in the chlorine atom.

The larger the dipole moment, the larger the attractive force. Dipole-dipole forces are **ELECTROSTATIC**.

Hydrogen Bonds

HYDROGEN BONDS are the strongest of the Van der Waals forces. Although it has the word *bond* in its name, a hydrogen bond is NOT an actual chemical bond. It is much weaker than an ionic, covalent, or even metallic bond.

Hydrogen bonds are the intermolecular forces between hydrogen (H) and fluorine (F), oxygen (O), or nitrogen (N).

When bonded to water, electrons are pulled toward the more electronegative fluorine (F), oxygen (O), or nitrogen (N) atoms, creating a small dipole.

Values for electron negativities (listed on the electronegativity chart) are:

F = 4.0   O = 3.4   N = 3.0   H = 2.2

When dipoles of two different molecules of ammonia (NH_3) line up (the hydrogen of one ammonia atom is on the same plane as the two electrons around the nitrogen atom in the ammonia molecule), a hydrogen bond is formed:

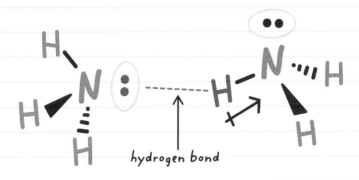

hydrogen bond

The black dashed lines show the bond at angles that are on a different plane to nitrogen. The black triangles show that the element is on a different plane, as though it's coming toward you. The red dashed line shows that the element is positioned toward the back. The circular shapes around the two sets of electrons show that they are bonded to each other and not to a hydrogen atom.

Hydrogen bonding only occurs with fluorine, oxygen, or nitrogen atoms.

INTERMOLECULAR FORCES AND STATES OF MATTER

Intermolecular forces play a part in the state in which an element is found.

There are three states of matter:

SOLIDS have strong intermolecular forces that keep particles locked into place, but the particles can still vibrate back and forth.

LIQUIDS have intermediate intermolecular forces that are strong enough to keep particles close but allow them to move about.

GASES have weak intermolecular forces, because the particles are spread out and can freely move as they wish.

In general,
Weaker forces = lower boiling points
                and melting points
Stronger forces = higher boiling points
                and melting points

FOR EXAMPLE: Which of the following substances has the lowest melting point? Which has the highest melting point?

NH₃   Ne   MgO

Magnesium oxide (MgO) is an ionic compound, because magnesium gives up two of its electrons to oxygen to form an ionic bond.

A strong electrostatic force of attraction exists among magnesium oxide molecules.

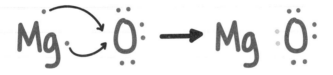

MgO is the compound with the highest melting point because it is an ionic compound.

Neon (Ne) is a noble gas and can only have London dispersion forces, the weakest intermolecular bonds. These are based on instantaneous dipoles, which are created by the movement of its electrons.

Ne has the weakest forces and the lowest boiling point.

You can also use the electronegativities chart to check the electronegativities of each element.

NH_3:   The electronegativity of N is 3.0.
            The electronegativity of H is 2.2.

$$3 - 2.2 = 0.8$$

This will be a dipole, because the difference is greater than 0.4.

This is the Lewis structure:

The H atoms are covalently bonded to the N atom, meaning the structure contains hydrogen bonds.

$$H - \overset{\cdot\cdot}{N} - H$$
$$|$$
$$H$$

NH_3 has a covalent bond and has a lower melting point than MgO.

CHECK YOUR KNOWLEDGE

1. What is a metallic bond and how is it formed?

2. Name three properties that determine the strength of a metallic bond.

3. What are the two types of forces that describe how atoms interact, and how do these forces differ?

4. Name the three types of intermolecular forces according to their increasing strength.

5. Define a dipole interaction and give an example of one molecule that may undergo a dipole interaction.

6. Between which two atoms can a hydrogen bond form?

ANSWERS ➡ 229

CHECK YOUR ANSWERS

1. Metallic bonds are formed when two metal atoms share the electrons between them. The bonds are created in an "electron sea."

2. The three properties determining the strength of a metallic bond are the number of electrons that are free to move about the metal, the charge of the cation (metal), and the cation size.

3. *Intramolecular* forces hold a molecule or compound together and form covalent, ionic, and metallic bonds. *Intermolecular* forces are weaker than intramolecular forces, occur between the molecules, and influence their physical properties, such as boiling point and melting point.

4. According to increasing strength, the three types of intermolecular forces are London dispersion, dipole-dipole interactions, and hydrogen bonding.

5. A dipole force is the attraction between the positive end of one polar molecule and the negative end of another polar molecule. Examples are HF and HCl.

6. Hydrogen bonds are the intermolecular forces between hydrogen and fluorine (F), oxygen (O), or nitrogen (N).

Unit 5

Chemical Compounds

Chapter 17

NAMING SUBSTANCES

Chemical substances are named according to **NOMENCLATURE** developed by scientists.

NOMENCLATURE
Rules for naming chemical compounds.

NAMING IONIC COMPOUNDS

Ionic compounds are formed when a metal cation (+) bonds with a nonmetal anion (−).

MONATOMIC IONS get their name from the elements.

MONATOMIC ION
An ion containing only one atom.

Rules for naming monatomic ions:

Cations: Add ion after the name of the element.

ELEMENT	CATION NAME	ION SYMBOL
Sodium (Na)	Sodium ion	Na^+
Potassium (K)	Potassium ion	K^+
Calcium (Ca)	Calcium ion	Ca^{2+}
Aluminum (Al)	Aluminum ion	Al^{3+}

Anions: Change the ending of the element name to *ide*, and add *ion* after it.

ELEMENT	ANION NAME	ION SYMBOL
Chlorine (Cl)	Chloride ion	Cl^-
Fluorine (F)	Fluoride ion	F^-
Sulfur (S)	Sulfide ion	S^{2-}
Phosphorous (P)	Phosphide ion	P^{3-}

The positive charge of a transition-metal ion can be written with Roman numerals (I, II, III, . . .) that are placed inside parentheses ( ) in the name. This is called the STOCK SYSTEM.

When you write an ion, you write its symbol and charge.

233

The Roman numerals match the number of the positive charge.

ELEMENT	ION SYMBOL	STOCK SYSTEM NAME
Copper (Cu)	Cu^+	Copper (I) ion
	Cu^{2+}	Copper (II) ion
Iron (Fe)	Fe^{2+}	Iron (II) ion
	Fe^{3+}	Iron (III) ion
Cobalt (Co)	Co^{2+}	Cobalt (II) ion
	Co^{3+}	Cobalt (III) ion
*Lead (Pb)	Pb^{2+}	Lead (II) ion
	Pb^{4+}	Lead (IV) ion
*Tin (Sn)	Sn^{2+}	Tin (II) ion
	Sn^{4+}	Tin (IV) ion

*Although lead and tin are not transition metals,
they still use Roman numerals in their names.

Some metals have more than one oxidation state, which means that they can form more than one ion. These are sometimes written with the original Latin endings to indicate the ion that has the higher oxidation state and the ion that has the lower oxidation state, given the two most common charges for that particular element.

Latin endings that indicate oxidation state:

ous = lower oxidation state; *ic* = higher oxidation state

ELEMENT	ION SYMBOL	STOCK SYSTEM	LATIN NAME
Copper (Cu)	Cu^+	Copper (I) ion	Cuprous ion
Copper (Cu)	Cu^{2+}	Copper (II) ion	Cupric ion
Iron (Fe)	Fe^{2+}	Iron (II) ion	Ferrous ion
Iron (Fe)	Fe^{3+}	Iron (III) ion	Ferric ion
Tin (Sn)	Sn^{2+}	Tin (II) ion	Stannous ion
Tin (Sn)	Sn^{4+}	Tin (IV) ion	Stannic ion

BINARY COMPOUNDS are created when two elements bond.

bi = two

> When a metal cation and a nonmetal anion bond together with an ionic bond,
>
> - name the metal first and the nonmetal second.
> - subtract the ending on the anion.
> - add *ide* to the ending.

BINARY COMPOUNDS			
COMPOUND	**METAL CATION**	**NONMETAL ANION**	**COMPOUND**
NaCl	Sodium	Chlorine	Sodium chloride
$CaBr_2$	Calcium	Bromine	Calcium bromide
Al_2O_3	Aluminum	Oxygen	Aluminum oxide
ZnI_2	Zinc	Iodine	Zinc iodide
CuF	Copper (I)	Fluorine	Copper (I) fluoride
CuF_2	Copper (II)	Fluorine	Copper (II) fluoride

WRITING FORMULAS FOR BINARY COMPOUNDS

What to know:

- Type of ion (is it a cation or anion?)

- Charge of ion

The information is in the periodic table, based on its position and group number.

- The total positive charge = the total negative charge in a neutral compound.

- The charge on the cation becomes the subscript on the anion.

- The charge on the anion becomes the subscript on the cation.

Use the CRISS-CROSS RULE:

subscript

The **subscript** is the number printed below the symbol (O_2).
The subscript tells how many atoms are in the compound.

Al^{3+} and O^{2-} Mg^{2+} and S^{2-}

$Al_2 O_3$ $Mg_2 S_2$

Reduce to the lowest terms.

Final formula: Al_2O_3 MgS (both 2s reduce to 1)

Names: Aluminum oxide   Magnesium sulfide

TERNARY COMPOUNDS

ter means "three"

A **TERNARY COMPOUND** is made up of **three or more** elements. For example,

a metal + a nonmetal + a nonmetal = ternary compound

poly: Greek for "many"

Two **POLYATOMIC IONS** may also form a ternary compound, such as ammonium nitrate (found in fertilizer). Polyatomic ions are ions that are formed from more than one element.

Examples of polyatomic ions:

Acetate	$C_2H_3O_2^-$	Sulfite	SO_3^{2-}
Ammonium	NH_4^+	Sulfate	SO_4^{2-}
Carbonate	CO_3^{2-}	Phosphite	PO_3^{3-}
Hypochlorite	ClO^-	Phosphate	PO_4^{3-}
Chlorite	ClO_2^-	Permanganate	MnO_4^-
Perchlorate	ClO_4^-	Iodate	IO_3^-
Nitrite	NO_2^-	Hydrogen carbonate	HCO_3^-
Nitrate	NO_3^-		

A **TERNARY SALT** is a compound made up of three different elements. A ternary salt is named according to the polyatomic ion with which it is bonded.

Naming and Writing Ternary Salts

- The first name is the metal ion.

- The second name is the nonmetal polyatomic ion.

- The **standard ending is –ate.**
  Metal ion + nonmetal polyatomic ion + ate

FOR EXAMPLE:

$Ca^{2+} + SO_4^{2-} \rightarrow CaSO_4$

Calcium ion + sulfate ion $\rightarrow$ calcium sulfate

$Sn^{2+} + NO_3^- \rightarrow Sn(NO_3)_2$ ⬅

Tin (II)/stannous ion + nitrate ion $\rightarrow$
stannous nitrate or tin (II) nitrate

Always place parentheses when more than one of a polyatomic ion is needed.
$Sn(NO_3)_2$, NOT $SnNO_{32}$

Things to know!

Sometimes, several polyatomic ions may be in the same family. Chlorine can form different states when bonded with oxygen to form ions:

- ClO_4^- is the **perchlorate** ion (**per** means "above" or more oxygen atoms than the "ate").

- ClO_3^- is the chlor**ate** ion.

- ClO_2^- is the chlor**ite** ion (one oxygen atom less than the most common).

- ClO^- is the **hypo**chlor**ite** ion (**hypo** means "below" or one oxygen atom less than the "ite").

> **States of polyatomic ions from greatest to least:**
> Per_ate > ate > ite > hypo__ite

TERNARY ACIDS are acids formed from hydrogen (H+) polyatomic ions.

Ternary acids use Latin endings to distinguish among oxidation levels:

A per___ate complex ion is named as a per___ic acid.

An -ate complex ion is named as an -ic acid.

An -ite complex ion is named as an -ous acid.

A hypo___ite complex ion is named as a hypo___ous acid.

For example:

$HClO_4$ contains the **per**chlor**ate** ion and is named **per**chlor**ic** acid.

$HClO_3$ contains the chlor**ate** ion and is named chlor**ic** acid.

$HClO_2$ contains the chlor**ite** ion and is named chlor**ous** acid.

HClO contains the **hypo**chlor**ite** ion and is named **hypo**chlor**ous** acid.

TERNARY BASES are metal ions that combine with the hydroxide (OH⁻) ion.

Ternary bases use an **-ide** ending.

For example,

$Ba^{2+} + OH^- \rightarrow Ba(OH)_2$

Barium ion + hydroxide ion → barium hydroxide

$Fe^{2+} + OH^- \rightarrow Fe(OH)_2$

Iron (II) OR ferrous ion + hydroxide → iron (II) hydroxide OR ferrous hydroxide

Note the parentheses around the hydroxide ion. Although there is no subscript at the H, you still need to add the parentheses. You cannot just add the 2 using the criss-cross rule. The polyatomic ion (OH⁻) must stay together with parentheses so that the overall total positive charge equals the overall total negative charge.

NAMING MOLECULAR COMPOUNDS

Molecular compounds occur when two nonmetals covalently bond with each other. Nonmetals tend to be close together on the right side of the periodic table.

Rules for naming nonmetal compounds:

1. Keep the first element's name as is.

2. Name the element with the higher electronegativity value second.

3. Add an **-ide** ending.

4. If more than one element is present in the compound, use a prefix to indicate the number of elements.

Mono = 1	Hexa = 6
Di = 2	Hepta = 7
Tri = 3	Octa = 8
Tetra = 4	Nona = 9
Penta = 5	Deca = 10

5. If there is only one of the first element, do not add the "mono" prefix.

6. If there are adjacent vowels that are the same, drop one of them.

FOR EXAMPLE: What is the name of the compound SiI_4?

Si is silicon. I is iodine.

Rule 1: Keep silicon as is.

Rule 2: Iodine has a higher electronegativity value than silicon, so list it second.

Rule 3: Add the **-ide** ending.

Rule 4: There are four iodine atoms, so it's **tetra iodine**.

Rule 5: There is only one silicon, so do not add the "mono" prefix.

Rule 6: Does not apply.

Answer: SiI_4 = **silicon tetraiodide**

1. What are the names of the following ions: Fe^{3+}, Pb^{2+}, Sn^{4+}, and S^{2-}?

2. What is the formula for permanganic acid?

3. What is the name of BCl_3?

4. Give the name of N_2O_4.

5. What is the name of the compound that the two ions Ca^{2+} and I^{1-} combine to form?

6. What is the formula for hypochlorous acid?

7. What is the formula for ferric hydroxide?

ANSWERS ➤ 247

1. Iron (III) ion OR ferric ion, lead (II) ion OR plumbous ion, tin (IV) ion OR stannic ion, and sulfide ion.

2. $HMnO_4$. Because it has a per___ic format, it's a ternary acid formed with hydrogen. The middle "mangan" is from the polyatomic ion manganate (MnO_4^-). The **-ic** ending means that it is at the current oxidation state.

3. Boron trichloride

4. Dinitrogen tetroxide

5. CaI_2: Calcium iodide

6. $HClO$. "Hypo" means that it contains a hypochlorite ion (ClO^-) attached to a hydrogen atom.

7. $Fe(OH)_3$. "Ferric" refers to Fe (III) or Fe^{3+} and the hydroxide polyatomic ion OH^-, of which three are needed to cancel out the +3 oxidation number of the iron (III).

Chapter 18

THE MOLE

Scientists use an International System of Units (SI) measurement called a **MOLE** to represent the number of particles in a substance. It would be impossible to measure each individual atom because they are so small.

The abbreviation for mole is **mol**.

MOLE
The SI base unit used to measure the amount of a substance. The number of carbon atoms in exactly 12.000 g of the carbon-12 isotope.

Why carbon-12? Carbon-12 has exactly six protons and six neutrons in its nucleus and is relatively easy to measure accurately every time. It was given the exact atomic mass of 12 and is used as the standard for all other atomic, molecular, and formulaic masses.

The number of atoms in 12 grams (g) of **carbon-12** is equal to Avogadro's number or 6.022×10^{23} atoms (or molecules).

Saying you have a mole of something—no matter what it is—means that you have 6.022×10^{23} (that's 602, 200, 000, 000, 000, 000, 000, 000) of it.

1 mol of pennies would cover the entire Earth for a depth of 0.3 miles.

Avogadro's number was not actually discovered by the credited Italian scientist AMEDEO AVOGADRO. Although he did propose the hypothesis that two samples of gas of equal volume at the same temperature and pressure would contain the same number of molecules. The hypothesis was accepted in 1811. But it wasn't until 1909, when French physicist JEAN BAPTISTE PERRIN first used the number in his experiment, that Avogadro's hypothesis was proven. Perrin named the number after Avogadro to recognize him for his scientific contribution.

ATOMIC AND MOLAR MASS

1 mol of carbon-12 has exactly 6.022×10^{23} atoms and a mass of 12 g. The mass in grams of carbon-12 is its **MOLAR MASS**.

The **ATOMIC MASS** of one atom of carbon-12 is 12 **ATOMIC MASS UNITS (AMU)**.

When calculating, always use the correct number of significant figures (sig figs) in the answer. Go by the number of sig figs in the least accurate number given.

> **MOLAR MASS**
> The mass (in grams) of 1 mol of units of a substance or grams/mole.
>
> **ATOMIC MASS**
> The mass of one atom expressed in atomic mass units.
>
> **ATOMIC MASS UNITS (AMU)**
> The mass that is exactly equal to $\frac{1}{12}$ of the mass of one carbon-12 atom.

For example: If a measurement is given to be 15 m, it is only accurate to two significant figures. Even if you use Avogadro's number when calculating, you must still report your answer using only two significant figures.

How do you use this information?

If you know the molar mass (given in the periodic table) and Avogadro's number, you can figure out the mass of a single atom in grams.

The molar mass relationship can be used as a conversion factor between moles and the number of atoms in a substance with these equations:

$$\frac{1 \text{ mol substance } Y}{\text{molar mass substance } Y} \quad \text{OR} \quad \frac{1 \text{ mol } Y}{6.022 \times 10^{23} \text{ atoms}}$$

Calculating Molecular Mass

Molecular mass is the sum of the atomic masses in the molecule and is given in atomic mass units (amu).

If you know the atomic mass of each element, you can use it to calculate molecular mass.

> When adding numbers, the rule for sig figs is to round to the least number of decimal places.

To calculate the molecular mass of water (H_2O), follow these steps:

1. Separate each element by number, based on the subscript to the right of each element.

H_2O has two hydrogen (H) atoms and one oxygen (O) atom.

2. Get the atomic mass for each element from the periodic table.

Atomic mass of H = 1.0078 amu
Atomic mass of O = 15.999 amu

3. Add them together. (You can also round to the hundredths place for easier calculation.)

The molecular mass is equal to the sum total of each atom present (in amu).

2 (atomic mass H) + 1 (atomic mass O) = molecular mass

2 (1.01 amu) + 1 (16.00 amu)

2.02 + 16.00 = 18.02 amu

> molar masses rounded to the hundredths place

FOR EXAMPLE: What is the molecular mass of glucose ($C_6H_{12}O_6$)?

6 (atomic mass of C) + 12 (atomic mass of H) + 6 (atomic mass of O) = molecular mass of $C_6H_{12}O_6$

6 (12.009 amu) + 12 (1.0078 amu) + 6 (15.999 amu) = 180.142 amu

The molecular mass of $C_6H_{12}O_6$ is 180.142 amu.

Calculating Moles

You can convert to find the amount of moles in a given substance.

WE'RE GOING TO NEED A LOT MORE CARTONS . . .

A dozen eggs   A mole of eggs

FOR EXAMPLE: If you have 15 g of magnesium (Mg) in a sample, how many moles of Mg atoms are in the sample?

Start with what you know.

You need to convert 15 g into moles.

1. Find the molar mass in the periodic table.

1 mol Mg = 24.305 g

> Green = numbers found in the periodic table
>
> Blue = numbers given in the problem
>
> Orange = Avogadro's number

2. Write the conversion factors.

$$\frac{1\ mol\ Mg}{24.305\ g} \quad OR \quad \frac{1\ mol\ Mg}{6.022 \times 10^{23}\ atoms}$$

3. The given number is in grams, so use the conversion factor on the left so that the units divide out (grams divided by grams = 1).

$$15\ g\ Mg \times \frac{1\ mol\ Mg}{24.305\ g\ Mg} = .62\ mol\ Mg \qquad \boxed{\frac{15 \times 1}{24.305} = \frac{15}{24.305} = .62}$$

The units of g Mg in the numerator will divide with the units of g Mg in the denominator, which will leave moles as the unit for the final answer.

Calculating Grams

You can convert to find the number of grams in a given substance.

FOR EXAMPLE: How many grams of iron (Fe) are in .850 mol of Fe?

Start with what you know.

Given number: .850 mol Fe

Convert .850 mol into grams.

1 mol Fe = 55.845 g (from the periodic table).

$$.850 \text{ mol Fe} \times \frac{55.845 \text{ g}}{1 \text{ mol Fe}} = 47.5 \text{ g Fe}$$

Calculating Atoms of One Element

Sometimes you need to convert twice to get to the requested unit. For example, from grams to moles to atoms.

FOR EXAMPLE: If you have 6.58 g of carbon, how many atoms of carbon are there?

1 mol C = 12.009 g

To find atoms, convert:

Grams of C to moles of C to atoms of C

$$6.58 \; g \; C \times \frac{1 \; mol \; C}{12.009 \; g \; C} \times \frac{6.022 \times 10^{23} \; atoms}{1 \; mol \; C}$$

$= 3.30 \times 10^{23}$ atoms of carbon

Calculating Atoms of One Element in a Compound

Sometimes, you need to know how many atoms of a single element are present in a compound. Each element in the compound has a subscript.

> The formula of a compound shows ONLY whole-number (integer) multiples of the moles, that is, 1, 2, 3, 4, 5. . . . It is not typical to have a fraction of a mole present in a chemical formula.

The subscript tells you how many moles of that element are present in the compound.

257

1 mol of CO_2 has 1 mol carbon atoms and 2 mol oxygen atoms.

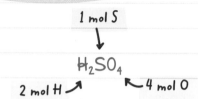

1 mol S

H_2SO_4

2 mol H

4 mol O

H_2SO_4 has 2 mol H, 1 mol S, and 4 mol O.

Once you know how many moles of an element are present in a compound, you can figure out how many atoms it may have.

FOR EXAMPLE: How many nitrogen (N) atoms are present in 32.68 g of caffeine ($C_8H_{10}N_4O_2$)?

1. Start with the given values and then make this conversion:

Grams of caffeine to moles of caffeine to moles of nitrogen to atoms of nitrogen

2. Calculate grams per mole of caffeine using the periodic table:

Grams of caffeine (given) = 32.68 g

8 (atomic mass of C) + 10 (atomic mass of H) + 4 (atomic mass of N) + 2 (atomic mass of O) = g/mol caffeine

8 (12.009) + 10 (1.0078) + 4 (14.006) + 2 (15.999) = 194.172 g/mol caffeine

3. Determine the number of moles of N present in 1 mol of caffeine.

The formula for caffeine is $C_8H_{10}N_4O_2$.

The subscript indicates that there are 4 mol of N in 1 mol of caffeine, so you have this conversion factor: $\dfrac{4 \text{ mol}}{1 \text{ mol } C_8H_{10}N_4O_2}$.

4. Put it all together into one equation. Divide units out as you go.

$$32.68 \text{ g } C_8H_{10}N_4O_2 \times \frac{1 \text{ mol } C_8H_{10}N_4O_2}{194.172 \text{ g } C_8H_{10}N_4O_2} \times \frac{4 \text{ mol N}}{1 \text{ mol}} \times$$

$$\frac{6.022 \times 10^{23} \text{ atoms}}{1 \text{ mol N}}$$

= 4.054×10^{23} atoms of N present in 32.68 g of the $C_8H_{10}N_4O_2$ compound

Using Molecular Mass to Calculate Moles or Atoms of a Compound from Grams

Natural gas is composed of methane (CH_4). If you have 7.52 g of methane, how many moles of CH_4 do you have?

1. You have 7.52 g but need to convert to moles. You must first calculate the molecular mass of CH_4:

(12.009 g C) + 4 (1.0078 g H) = 16.040 g, the molecular mass of CH_4

2. Write the conversion factor: $\dfrac{1 \text{ mol } CH_4}{16.040 \text{ g } CH_4}$

3. Complete the calculation:

$7.52 \text{ g } CH_4 \times \dfrac{1 \text{ mol } CH_4}{16.040 \text{ g } CH_4} = .469 \text{ mol } CH_4$

4. To calculate the number of atoms:

$.469 \text{ mol } CH_4 \times \dfrac{6.022 \times 10^{23} \text{ atoms}}{1 \text{ mol } CH_4} = 2.82 \times 10^{23} \text{ atoms of } CH_4$

CHECK YOUR KNOWLEDGE

1. How many atoms are in 1 mol of any substance?

2. What is the difference between molar mass and atomic mass?

3. How many atoms are in 4.65 mol of chromium (Cr)?

4. How many atoms are in .781 g of glucose ($C_6H_{12}O_6$)?

5. Calculate the molecular mass of Mg_3N_2.

6. How many moles of ethane (C_2H_6) are in 56.2 g of ethane?

ANSWERS 261

CHECK YOUR ANSWERS

1. The number of atoms in 1 mol of any substance is equal to Avogadro's number or 6.022×10^{23} atoms (or molecules, if it is a compound). This value is often stated using three significant figures: 6.02×10^{23}.

2. Molar mass is the mass (in grams) of 1 mol of units of a substance or grams/mole. Atomic mass is the mass of one atom expressed in atomic mass units.

3. $(4.65 \text{ mol}) (6.022 \times 10^{23} \text{ atoms/mol}) = 2.80 \times 10^{24}$ atoms

4. $(.781 \text{ g}/180.18 \text{ g/mol}) (6.022 \times 10^{23} \text{ atoms/mol})$
   $= 2.61 \times 10^{21}$ atoms

5. $3 (24.31 \text{ g}) + 2 (14.01 \text{ g}) = 100.95$ g/mol

6. $56.2 \text{ g}/30.08 \text{ g/mol} = 1.87$ moles

Chapter 19

FINDING COMPOSITIONS IN COMPOUNDS

COMPOSITIONS BY MASS

To find the purity of a compound or the amount of all of the different elements, by percentage, scientists calculate the **PERCENT COMPOSITION BY MASS**.

To calculate the percentage of brown eggs present, divide the number of brown eggs (4) by the total number of eggs (12).

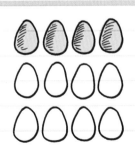

$4 \div 12 = .33$

33% of eggs are brown.

To find the percent composition,

1. Divide the mass of each element in 1 mol of the compound by the molar mass of the compound.

2. Multiply by 100%.

3. Give the answer in mass (grams).

The formula to find percent composition is:

$$\% \text{ Composition of element} = \frac{n \times \text{molar mass of element}}{\text{molar mass of compound}} \times 100\%,$$

where n is the number of atoms of the element in 1 mol of the compound.

FOR EXAMPLE: Ammonium nitrate (NH_4NO_3) is used as a fertilizer to add nitrogen to soil. Calculate the percent composition by mass of N, H, and O in the compound.

1. Determine the number of moles of each element in the compound from the subscripts:

N = 2 (The two individual Ns (subscripts of 1) combine to make a total of 2 mol.)

H = 4

O = 3

2. Add the molar mass of NH_4NO_3 using the information in the periodic table:

4 (1.008 g) + 3 (15.999 g) + 2 (14.006 g) = molar mass of NH_4NO_3 in g/mol

4.032 g H + 47.997 g O + 28.012 g N = 80.041 g/mol, the molar mass of NH_4NO_3

3. Calculate the percent composition for each element:

The amount of H present in the compound.

% Composition of H = $\dfrac{4\ (1.008\ g)}{80.041\ g}$ × 100% = 5.037% H

molar mass of compound

% Composition of O = $\dfrac{3\ (15.999\ g)}{80.041\ g}$ × 100% = 59.966% O

% composition of N = $\dfrac{2\ (14.006\ g)}{80.041\ g}$ × 100% = 34.997 % N

Hint:
Add all of the percentages of each element to make sure they come up to approximately 100%.

Determining Percentage of a Single Element in a Compound

Sometimes, scientists need to know the percentage of a single element that is found within the whole compound.

FOR EXAMPLE: Determine the percentage of oxygen in water (H_2O).

1. Calculate the molar mass values (periodic table):

O = 15.999 g/mol, H = 1.008 g/mol, H_2O = 18.015 g/mol

2. Calculate the percent of the element:

$$\% \; O = \frac{\text{molar mass of } O}{\text{molar mass of } H_2O} \times 100\%$$

$$\frac{15.999 \text{ g/mol } O}{18.015 \text{ g/mol } H_2O} \times 100\% = 88.81\%$$

The percentage of oxygen in water = 88.81%

FOR EXAMPLE: The formula for rust is Fe_2O_3. How many grams of iron (Fe) are in 22.8 g of rust?

1. Calculate the percentage of iron (Fe) that is in the rust using molar mass values listed in the periodic table:

$$\% \text{ Fe} = \frac{\text{molar mass of all Fe}}{\text{molar mass of } Fe_2O_3} \times 100\%$$

$$\frac{2(55.85 \text{ g/mol Fe})}{159.697 \text{ g/mol } Fe_2O_3} \times 100\% = 69.94\%$$

2. Calculate the grams of Fe in the 22.8 g sample of rust:

Multiply the mass of the rust by 69.94%:

22.8 g × 0.699 = 15.9 g of Fe in Fe_2O_3

Don't forget to include the zero to show 3 sig figs.

The mass percentage of an element in a compound is always calculated by

$$\frac{\text{total molar mass of the element in the compound}}{\text{molar mass of the compound}} \times 100$$

Don't forget to add all of the atoms of the element to get the numerator.

FINDING THE
EMPIRICAL FORMULA

An **EMPIRICAL FORMULA** of a compound is determined by the simplest whole-number ratio of every atom in the compound.

> ## EMPIRICAL FORMULA
> A formula showing the proportions of an element present in a compound.

FOR EXAMPLE: CH_2 is the simplest ratio of C_2H_4. The ratio of the subscripts 2:4 is simplified to 1:2. The empirical formula is sometimes, but not always, the same as the molecular formula. It's calculated using the percent composition of the compound.

FOR EXAMPLE: What is the empirical formula of a compound with the following percent compositions?

18.4% C, 21.5 % N, 60.1% K

1. Suppose you have a 100 g sample of the compound. This means that there is

18.4 g C, 21.5 g N, and 60.1 g K in that compound.

2. Convert grams of the element to moles of the element using the molar masses.

$$18.4 \text{ g C} \times \frac{1 \text{ mol C}}{12.01 \text{ g}} = 1.53 \text{ mol C}$$

molar mass from periodic table

$$21.5 \text{ g N} \times \frac{1 \text{ mol N}}{14.01 \text{ g}} = 1.53 \text{ mol N}$$

$$60.1 \text{ g K} \times \frac{1 \text{ mol K}}{39.1 \text{ g}} = 1.54 \text{ mol K}$$

3. Divide each mole value by the lowest number of moles listed.

A chemical formula shows only whole-number integers.

Divide each mol value by the lowest number: 1.53 mol.

Round to the nearest whole number.

$$\frac{1.53}{1.53} = 1$$

$$\frac{1.53}{1.53} = 1$$

$$\frac{1.54}{1.53} = 1.01,$$ which rounds to 1

4. Write the empirical formula using whole-number integers.

The final empirical formula is $K_1C_1N_1$ = KCN.

CHECK YOUR KNOWLEDGE

1. What is the percent composition of a compound and why is it important?

2. What is the process for finding percent composition?

3. What does the empirical formula mean?

4. What percent of oxygen is present in 5.6 g of adrenaline $(C_9H_{13}NO_3)$?

ANSWERS

CHECK YOUR ANSWERS

1. Percent composition of a compound is the percent by mass of each element in that compound. Scientists use percent composition to determine the purity of a compound or the amount of all of the different elements by percentage.

2. $$\frac{\% \text{ Composition of}}{\text{an element}} = \frac{n \times \text{molar mass of element}}{\text{molar mass of compound}} \times 100\%$$

3. The empirical formula gives the simplest whole-number ratio of atoms in a compound.

4. 3 (15.999)/[9 (12.01) + 13 (1.008) + 14.01 + 3 (15.999)] × 100
   = 26.20%

   .2620 × 5.6 = 1.5 g O

Unit 7

Chemical Reactions and Calculations

Chapter 20

CHEMICAL REACTIONS

CHEMICAL REACTIONS

When chemicals combine, they make a new substance. This process of combining substances is called a **CHEMICAL REACTION**. During a chemical reaction, two or more substances called **REACTANTS** interact, or have an effect on one another. The bonds between their atoms are broken, and new bonds are created, forming new substances.

> **CHEMICAL REACTION**
> A process during which substances are changed into one or more new substances.

Chemical reactions can show up in different ways, and they leave evidence of occurring.

Evidence of a chemical reaction can be:

- a change in color
- the creation of a solid (precipitate is formed)
- the release of light
- the formation of a gas
- a change in temperature

When a chemical reaction happens, scientists ask:

- How did the substances react?
- How did the reactants change?

Scientists use **CHEMICAL EQUATIONS** to represent the changes that occur when chemicals react.

A chemical equation is the symbolic representation of a chemical reaction. Chemical equations use CHEMICAL SYMBOLS (the same as those in the periodic table) to name each element.

The first chemical equation was written by JEAN BEGUIN in 1615.

Instead of an "=" sign, chemical equations use an arrow (→) called a YIELD SIGN.

The chemicals on the left side of the yield sign are called the **REACTANTS**. Chemicals on the right of the yield sign are called the **PRODUCTS**. The "+" sign means "reacts with." The arrow indicates that a reaction is taking place (bonds are breaking and reforming) and is read as "yields."

reactant + reactant → products

The number preceding the chemical symbol, the coefficient, tells the number of moles in that substance.

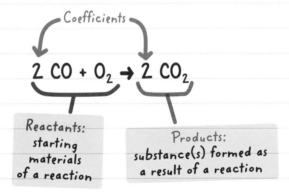

Coefficients

$$2\ CO + O_2 \rightarrow 2\ CO_2$$

Reactants: starting materials of a reaction

Products: substance(s) formed as a result of a reaction

This chemical equation is read as **carbon monoxide (CO) reacts with oxygen (O) to yield carbon dioxide (CO_2).**

The number of moles of a substance is indicated by the number in front of the element/molecule. No number means 1 mole. In the equation $2\ CO + O_2 \rightarrow 2\ CO_2$: 2 mol CO react with 1 mol O_2, yielding 2 mol CO_2.

Chemical equations follow the LAW OF CONSERVATION OF MASS.

This means that chemical equations must be balanced.

> The number of moles of each element on the left side of the equation must equal the number of moles of the element on the right side of the equation.

BALANCING CHEMICAL EQUATIONS

A balanced chemical equation happens when the number of the different atoms of elements on the reactants side is equal to the number of atoms on the products side. The equation has the same number of each type of atom on both sides.

Balancing chemical equations involves trial and error.

Steps for balancing chemical equations:

1. Look for multiples of the coefficient.

You can only change the number of molecules, not the molecule itself. This means change only the coefficient, not the subscript.

For example, hydrogen can react with oxygen to form water. If you have twos, try to double that number to a four.

$$H_2 + O_2 \rightarrow H_2O$$

can be balanced as

$$2H_2 + O_2 \rightarrow 2H_2O$$

Find coefficients that give equal numbers of each type of atom.

2. Write the unbalanced equation.

For example, hydrogen (H_2) reacting with oxygen (O_2) yields water (H_2O):

$$H_2 + O_2 \rightarrow H_2O$$

3. Count the number of moles of each element on both sides of the equation:

$$\text{reactants} \rightarrow \text{products}$$

$$H_2 + O_2 \rightarrow H_2O$$

H = 2	H = 2
O = 2	O = 1

4. Ask yourself whether the number of moles on each side are equal.

Are the number of moles on each side equal?

No → Balance the equation: (Step 5)

Yes → The equation is balanced.

2 mol H = 2 mol H   balanced

2 mol O ≠ 1 mol O   not balanced

The equation is not balanced.

5. Multiply the element or compound, whose value is too small, by enough to equal the particles on the other side.

$$H_2 + O_2 \rightarrow H_2O$$
$$H_2 = H_2$$
$$O_2 \neq O$$

- Multiply H_2O by 2.

$$H_2 + O_2 \rightarrow 2H_2O$$

- That yields 2 H on the left and 4 H on the right, and 2 O on the left and 2 O on the right.

$$H_2 + O_2 \rightarrow 2H_2O$$

- Multiply the H_2 in the reactant by 2 to get 4 H on the left and 4 H on the right.

The balanced equation is $2H_2 + O_2 \rightarrow 2H_2O$.

$$2H_2 + O_2 \rightarrow 2H_2O$$

$$H = 2 \times 2 = 4 \quad | \quad H = 2 \times 2 = 4$$
$$O = 2 \quad | \quad O = 1 \times 2 = 2$$

6. Check. Count the number of moles of the elements on both sides of the equation. (Remember that the coefficients multiply.)

$2H_2 + O_2 \rightarrow 2H_2O$

$2H_2O$

4 mol H — 2 mol O

The equation is balanced.

The unbalanced chemical equation can be drawn like this:

$H_2 + O_2 \rightarrow H_2O$

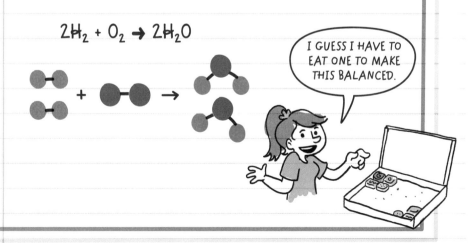

The balanced equation can be drawn like this:

$2H_2 + O_2 \rightarrow 2H_2O$

I GUESS I HAVE TO EAT ONE TO MAKE THIS BALANCED.

TYPES OF CHEMICAL REACTIONS

SYNTHESIS: Two or more substances combine to make one new product.

$$A + B \rightarrow AB$$

FOR EXAMPLE: $H_2 + Br_2 \rightarrow 2HBr$

1 mol hydrogen reacts with 1 mol bromine and yields 2 mol hydrogen bromide.

DECOMPOSITION: One substance breaks apart into two or more different products. Decomposition is the *opposite* of a synthesis reaction.

$$AB \rightarrow A + B$$

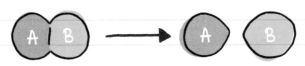

FOR EXAMPLE: $2HgO \rightarrow 2Hg + O_2$

2 mol mercury oxide decompose to 2 mol mercury and 1 mol molecular oxygen.

SINGLE REPLACEMENT: One element in a compound is replaced by another element. Elements that tend to form cations will replace the cation in a compound. Elements that tend to form anions will replace the anion in a compound.

$$AB + C \rightarrow A + BC$$

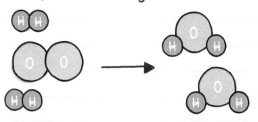

FOR EXAMPLE: $ZnCl_2 + Cu \rightarrow CuCl_2 + Zn$

1 mol zinc chloride combines with 1 mol copper to yield 1 mol copper (II) chloride and 1 mol zinc.

COMBUSTION: Oxygen reacts with all other elements in the original compound, forming oxides.

FOR EXAMPLE: $CH_4 + 2O_2 \rightarrow CO_2 + 2H_2O$

(This usually occurs when a hydrocarbon reacts with oxygen to produce a carbon dioxide and water.)

DOUBLE REPLACEMENT/METATHESIS: Two compounds react in an (aqueous) solution, and the cations and anions of the two reactants "switch places" to form two new compounds or products.

water

$$AB + CD \rightarrow AD + BC$$

FOR EXAMPLE: $AgSO_4 + 2NaCl \rightarrow AgCl_2 + Na_2SO_4$

Silver sulphate reacts with sodium chloride in an aqueous solution to yield silver chloride.

REDOX REACTIONS: This is the transfer of electrons between two substances. In this type of chemical reaction, the oxidation states of an atom, ion, or molecule changes during the course of the reaction.

FOR EXAMPLE: $Zn + 2H^+ \rightarrow Zn^{2+} + H_2$

Zn is oxidized (oxidation number: $0 \rightarrow +2$).
H+ is reduced (oxidation number: $+1 \rightarrow 0$).

PHYSICAL STATES OF REACTANTS AND PRODUCTS

Sometimes, it is helpful to know the physical state of a substance in an equation. Are the reactants solids? Liquids? Gases? In what state is the product?

It is helpful to know the states of the reactants, because elements and compounds are available in different states. You must pick the right state to get the product that you want to produce.

We use a subscript to show the physical state of a substance in a chemical equation.

(s) = solid

(l) = liquid

(g) = gas

(aq) = aqueous
     (present in water)

> The type of subscript that is used to show the physical state is different from the subscript in a compound. This subscript is a letter in parentheses, not a number.

For example, in this equation, the reactants and products are all in the **gas** state.

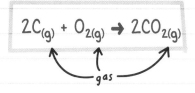

$$2C_{(g)} + O_{2(g)} \rightarrow 2CO_{2(g)}$$

gas

FOR EXAMPLE: Potassium bromide reacts best with silver nitrate if they are both in aqueous form (dissolved in water).

$$KBr_{(aq)} + AgNO_{3(aq)} \rightarrow KNO_{3(aq)} + AgBr_{(s)}$$

The chemical equation shows that:

- the reactants are in an aqueous form.

- the product contains both aqueous and solid elements.

CHECK YOUR KNOWLEDGE

1. Why do scientists use chemical equations?

2. What does it mean for a chemical equation to be balanced?

3. What is the difference between a chemical reaction and a chemical equation?

4. What are the main types of chemical reactions?

5. What type of reaction is occurring in each of these?
   A. $CaCl_2 + 2NaNO_3 \rightarrow 2NaCl + CaNO_3$
   B. $NH_4NO_2 \rightarrow N_2 + 2H_2O$
   C. $CH_4 + 2O_2 \rightarrow CO_2 + 2H_2O$

6. Balance the following equations:
   A. $NaHCO_3 \rightarrow Na_2CO_3 + H_2O + CO_2$
   B. $Cu + HNO_3 \rightarrow Cu(NO_3)_2 + NO + H_2O$
   C. $P_4O_{10} + H_2O \rightarrow H_3PO_4$

7. Why is it important to know the physical state of the reactants and the products?

8. What does *aqueous* mean?

ANSWERS ⟩ 287

CHECK YOUR ANSWERS

1. Scientists use chemical equations to represent the changes that occur between chemicals when they react.

2. For the chemical equation to be balanced, the number of moles of each element on the left side of the equation is equal to the number of moles of the element on the right side of the equation.

3. A chemical reaction is a process in which reactants are changed into products. A chemical equation uses chemical symbols to represent that process.

4. The main types of chemical reactions are synthesis, single replacement, decomposition, double replacement, redox, and combustion.

5. A. Double replacement
   B. Decomposition
   C. Combustion

6. A. $2NaHCO_3 \rightarrow Na_2CO_3 + H_2O + CO_2$
   B. $3Cu + 8HNO_3 \rightarrow 3Cu(NO_3)_2 + 2NO + 4H_2O$
   C. $P_4O_{10} + 6H_2O \rightarrow 4H_3PO_4$

7. It is important to know the physical state of the reactants and the products because this lets you know how the experiment was actually carried out.

8. *Aqueous* means that a substance has been dissolved in water.

Chapter 21

CHEMICAL CALCULATIONS

Scientists perform chemical calculations, or
STOICHIOMETRY, to measure the amount of reactants
and products in a chemical reaction. Stoichiometry answers
these questions:

■ How much product will be formed when specific
  amounts of the reactants combine?

■ How much of the reactants are required to create
  a specific amount of product(s)?

> **STOICHIOMETRY**
> The calculation of reactants and
> products in a chemical reaction
> (pronounced **stoy·kee·aa·muh·tree**).

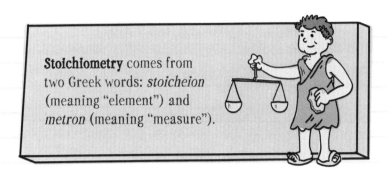

Stoichiometry comes from
two Greek words: *stoicheion*
(meaning "element") and
metron (meaning "measure").

Mole-to-Mole Stoichiometry

In mole-to-mole stoichiometry, we start with moles and end
with moles. The coefficients of each substance in a reaction
are represented by moles.

That means that in the equation $N_2 + 3H_2 \rightarrow 2NH_3$ there are

3 mol H_2

2 mol NH_3

1 mol N_2

This equation is read as *1 mol of nitrogen gas combines with
3 mol of hydrogen gas to form 2 mol of ammonia gas.*

The ratios in the equation can be written as

$$\frac{3 \text{ mol } H_2}{2 \text{ mol } NH_3} \quad \text{OR} \quad \frac{2 \text{ mol } NH_3}{3 \text{ mol } H_2} \quad \text{OR} \quad \frac{1 \text{ mol } N_2}{2 \text{ mol } NH_3} \quad \text{OR} \quad \frac{2 \text{ mol } NH_3}{1 \text{ mol } N_2}$$

These ratios can be used in calculations with **DIMENSIONAL
ANALYSIS**.

FOR EXAMPLE: In the equation $N_2 + 3H_2 \rightarrow 2NH_3$, how many moles of NH_3 will be produced when 4.0 mol H_2 reacts completely with N_2?

Solve the problem by multiplying the given information by a ratio from the chemical reaction.

Moles of NH_3 produced:

$$4.0 \text{ mol } H_2 \times \frac{2 \text{ mol } NH_3}{3 \text{ mol } H_2} = 2.7 \text{ mol } NH_3$$

Mass-to-Mass Stoichiometry
In these calculations reactants and products are given in mass. Questions like this are asked:

"Given x amount of reactant, how much product will form?"

You can take the equation $N_2 + 3H_2 \rightarrow 2NH_3$ one step further to calculate the grams of NH_3 produced, by using the grams in 1 mol NH_3 (found in the periodic table):

Grams in 1 mol NH_3: 14.01 g N + 3 (1.008 g H) = 17.03 g

$$2.7 \text{ mol } NH_3 \times \frac{17.03 \text{ g}}{1 \text{ mol } NH_3} = 46 \text{ g of } NH_3 \text{ produced}$$

To solve mass-to-mass stoichiometry problems:

1. Write a balanced equation for the chemical reaction.

2. Start with the mass of the reactant given in the problem. Convert the amount of reactant to number of moles.

> Mass of Reactant → Mole Reactant

3. Use the mole ratio from the balanced equation to convert to the moles of product created.

> Mole Reactant → Mole Product

4. Convert the moles of product to grams of product.

> Mole Product → Mass Product

You don't actually calculate each section of the problem individually; instead, you calculate the entire problem as a whole.

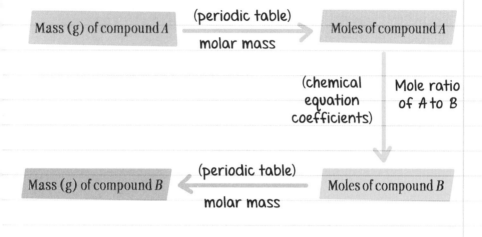

Mass (g) of compound A ──(periodic table) molar mass──▶ Moles of compound A

(chemical equation coefficients)   Mole ratio of A to B

Mass (g) of compound B ◀──(periodic table) molar mass── Moles of compound B

mass A → mole A → mole B → mass B

FOR EXAMPLE: Butane, a hydrocarbon (C_4H_{10}), undergoes combustion to produce carbon dioxide and water.

With 236.5 g butane, how many grams of carbon dioxide are formed in the reaction?

1. Write a balanced equation.

This combustion reaction involves a hydrocarbon, which means that oxygen (O_2) is a reactant and carbon dioxide (CO_2) and water (H_2O) are the products.

$C_4H_{10} + O_2 \rightarrow CO_2 + H_2O$

The balanced equation is

$$2C_4H_{10} + 13O_2 \rightarrow 8CO_2 + 10H_2O$$

2. Convert the amount of butane to moles.

Calculate the molar mass of butane.

C_4H_{10} molar mass = 4 (12.01 g) C + 10 (1.008 g) H = 58.12 g

$$236.5 \text{ g butane} \times \frac{1 \text{ mol butane}}{58.12 \text{ g}} = 4.069 \text{ mol butane}$$

3. Use the mole to calculate the moles of CO_2.

Get the mole ratio from the equation 2 mol butane = 8 mol carbon dioxide:

$$4.069 \text{ mol butane} \times \frac{8 \text{ mol carbon dioxide}}{2 \text{ mol butane}} = 16.27 \text{ mol } CO_2$$

4. Convert moles to grams of product.

Calculate molar mass of carbon dioxide.

CO_2 molar mass = 1(12.01g) C + 2 (15.999) O = 44.01 g

$$16.27 \text{ mol } CO_2 \times \frac{44.01 \text{ g } CO_2}{1 \text{ mol } CO_2} = 716.0 \text{ g } CO_2$$

716.0 g CO_2 is created from 236.5 g of butane

To calculate the atoms of CO_2, multiply the number of moles of CO_2 by Avogadro's number:

$16.27 \text{ mol } CO_2 \times \dfrac{6.022 \times 10^{23} \text{ atoms}}{1 \text{ mol } CO_2} = 9.798 \times 10^{24} \text{ atoms of } CO_2$

FOR EXAMPLE: Hydrogen sulfide gas burns in oxygen to produce sulfur dioxide and water. With 56.2 g of oxygen for this combustion reaction, how many grams of water will the reaction produce?

Balanced equation: $2H_2S + 3O_2 \rightarrow 2SO_2 + 2H_2O$

Known information:

There are 56.2 g O_2 (information given)
O_2 = 32.00 g/mol (from the periodic table)
H_2O = 18.02 g/mol (from the periodic table)

Conversion factor: g $O_2 \rightarrow$ mol $O_2 \rightarrow$ mol $H_2O \rightarrow$ g H_2O

$56.2 \text{ g } O_2 \times \dfrac{1 \text{ mol } O_2}{32.00 \text{ g } O_2} \times \dfrac{2 \text{ mol } H_2O}{3 \text{ mol } O_2} \times \dfrac{18.02 \text{ g } H_2O}{1 \text{ mol } H_2O} = 21.1 \text{ g } H_2O \text{ produced}$

Mass-to-Volume Stoichiometry

Sometimes in gas reactants or products, the measurements may be given in volume, not mass.

> **Standard temperature and pressure (STP) =**
> **zero degrees Celsius (0°C) or**
> **273 Kelvin (K) and 1 atmosphere (atm)**

At STP, this conversion factor is true for gases:

1 mol any gas = 22.4 L (L = liter)   OR

$$\frac{1 \text{ mol any gas}}{22.4 \text{ L}} \quad \text{OR} \quad \frac{22.4 \text{ L}}{1 \text{ mol any gas}}$$

> The molar volume of a gas at STP is equal to 22.4 L for 1 mol of any ideal gas at a temperature equal to 273.15 K and a pressure equal to 1.00 atm.

> **IDEAL GAS**
> A theoretical gas that consistently obeys the gas laws.

To solve mass-to-volume stoichiometry problems:

1. Write a balanced chemical equation for the reaction.

2. Convert amount of reactant to number of moles.

3. Use the mole ratio from the balanced equation to convert the amount (in moles) of product created.

4. Convert the moles of product to liters of product using the STP conversion factor for gases.

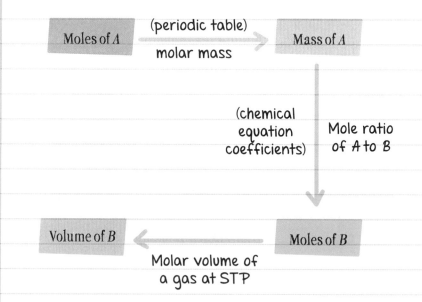

Magnesium reacts with hydrochloric acid, producing gas and magnesium chloride.

What volume of gas at STP is produced in this reaction when 54.6 g of HCl and abundant Mg are present?

Write the balanced equation:

Initial equation: $Mg_{(s)} + HCl \rightarrow MgCl_2 + H_{2(g)}$

Balanced equation: $Mg_{(s)} + 2HCl \rightarrow MgCl_2 + H_{2(g)}$

Molar mass of HCl = 1(1.008 g) H + 1(35.45g) Cl = 36.46 g HCl

Volume of H_2 generated: $54.6 \text{ g HCl} \times \dfrac{1 \text{ mol HCl}}{36.46 \text{ g HCl}} \times \dfrac{1 \text{ mol } H_2}{2 \text{ mol HCl}}$

$$\times \dfrac{22.4 \text{ L gas}}{1 \text{ mol } H_2} = 16.8 \text{ L}$$

FOR EXAMPLE: Convert from volume to mass:

12.3 L of H_2 gas is created when zinc is added to sulfuric acid. How much zinc, in mass, is needed for this reaction when it occurs at STP?

Known: 12.3 L H_2 gas

Sulfuric acid = H_2SO_4 = 98.08 g/mol

Zinc = Zn = 65.38 g/mol

H_2 = 2.01 g/mol

1 mol of gas at STP = 22.4 L/mol

Balanced equation: $Zn + H_2SO_4 \rightarrow H_2 + ZnSO_4$

Conversion: L of $H_2 \rightarrow$ mol $H_2 \rightarrow$ mole ratio of H_2 to Zn $\rightarrow$ g Zn

$$12.3 \text{ L } H_2 \times \frac{1 \text{ mol } H_2}{22.4 \text{ L}} \times \frac{1 \text{ mol } Zn}{1 \text{ mol } H_2} \times \frac{65.38 \text{ g } Zn}{1 \text{ mol } Zn} = 35.9 \text{ g of } Zn \text{ is needed}$$

Volume-to-Volume Stoichiometry

Equal volumes of all gases are the same at standard temperature and pressure (STP). You can get the volume ratios from the balanced equation.

FOR EXAMPLE: 36.3 L of oxygen react with ammonia to produce nitrogen gas and water at STP. What volume of nitrogen gas (in liters) will be produced?

1. Write the balanced equation.

$3O_2 + 4NH_3 \rightarrow 2N_2 + 6H_2O$

2. Write what is known:

36.3 L O_2
1 mol of gas = 22.4 L

3. Write the conversion factor.

L O_2 → mol O_2 → mol N_2 → liter N_2

4. Write and solve the equation.

$$36.3 \text{ L } O_2 \times \frac{1 \text{ mol } O_2}{22.4 \text{ L}} \times \frac{2 \text{ mol } N_2}{3 \text{ mol } O_2} \times \frac{22.4 \text{ L } N_2}{1 \text{ mol } N_2} = 24.2 \text{ (2 sig figs) L } N_2 \text{ is produced}$$

LIMITING REAGENTS

When carrying out a reaction, you must use the number of reactants that you have available. Sometimes, what you have does not equal the exact proportions in the equation. You may have less of a certain reactant. The reactant that is used up first in a chemical reaction is called the **LIMITING REAGENT**.

In a chemical reaction, not having enough of a reactant limits the amount of product that can be made.

FOR EXAMPLE: Suppose that you have a recipe that makes 12 cupcakes, but you need 36 cupcakes for a party. You will need to triple the ingredients for the recipe to get enough (or make the recipe three times).

Suppose that you need two eggs for each set of 12 cupcakes and you only have five eggs. When you've used up all the eggs (assuming you don't get more), your "reaction" is over. No more cupcakes.

Use balanced equations and stoichiometry to identify the limiting reagent.

FOR EXAMPLE: A reaction creates methanol (CH_3OH) from carbon monoxide and hydrogen gases. There are 3 mol CO and 8 mol H_2. Which is the limiting reagent?

1. Write the balanced equation.

$CO + 2H_2 \rightarrow CH_3OH$

2. Using the amount of moles given for each reactant, calculate how many moles of methanol will be produced.

$3 \text{ mol } CO \times \dfrac{1 \text{ mol } CH_3OH}{1 \text{ mol } CO} = 3 \text{ mol } CH_3OH$ produced

$8 \text{ mol } H_2 \times \dfrac{1 \text{ mol } CH_3OH}{2 \text{ mol } H_2} = 4 \text{ mol } CH_3OH$ produced

3. Identify the limiting reagent.

Because CO will produce less CH_3OH, it is the limiting reagent.

That makes H_2 the excess reagent.

Percent Yield

Once you know the limiting reagent, you can calculate the yield of the product(s). The yield, or amount, of the product produced if ALL of the limiting reagent was used up is called the **THEORETICAL YIELD**.

In reactions occurring in an actual lab where there are experimental errors, it is normal for some of the reagents to remain unused. So, we can calculate the **ACTUAL YIELD**.

Why is the actual yield unequal to the theoretical yield?
Sometimes the reagents didn't completely mix, the temperature wasn't high enough, or some of the reagent stuck to the side of the beaker. Some reactions are reversible, so reactants re-form over the course of the reaction.
The actual yield is usually less than the theoretical yield.

To find out the efficiency of the reaction on a scale of 1 to 100, scientists determine the **PERCENT YIELD**.

$$\% \text{ yield} = \frac{\text{actual yield}}{\text{theoretical yield}} \times 100\%$$

To calculate the percent yield of a reaction:

1. Write the balanced equation.

2. Calculate the theoretical yield of the product from the amount of the reactant given.

THEORETICAL YIELD
Amount of product that would be produced if the limiting reagent completely reacted.

ACTUAL YIELD
Amount of product actually produced in a reaction.

PERCENT YIELD
Ratio of actual yield to theoretical yield.

If you are given the amount of each reactant, calculate the limiting reactant. Use that amount to calculate the theoretical yield of the product.

3. Use the actual yield given and the theoretical yield that you calculated to determine the percent yield.

FOR EXAMPLE: Calcium fluoride (CaF_2) reacts with sulfuric acid (H_2SO_4) to produce calcium sulfate ($CaSO_4$) and hydrogen fluoride (HF). 56 g of sulfuric acid reacts with 85 g of calcium fluoride to produce 15 g of hydrogen fluoride. What is the percent yield of hydrogen fluoride (HF)?

1. Write the balanced equation.

$CaF_2 + H_2SO_4 \rightarrow CaSO_4 + 2HF$

2. Calculate the limiting reagent in grams (because you have the amounts of both of the reactants).

Known:
56 g H_2SO_4 and 1 mol H_2SO_4 = 98.08 g (from the periodic table)

85 g CaF_2 and 1 mol CaF_2 = 78.08 g (from the periodic table)

1 mol HF = 20.01 g (from the periodic table)

$$56 \text{ g } H_2SO_4 \times \frac{1 \text{ mol } H_2SO_4}{98.08 \text{ g } H_2SO_4} \times \frac{2 \text{ mol HF}}{1 \text{ mol } H_2SO_4} \times \frac{20.01 \text{ g HF}}{1 \text{ mol HF}}$$

$$= 22.84 \text{ g HF} = 23 \text{ g HF (2 sig fig)}$$

$$85 \text{ g } CaF_2 \times \frac{1 \text{ mol } CaF_2}{78.08 \text{ g}} \times \frac{2 \text{ mol HF}}{1 \text{ mol } CaF_2} \times \frac{20.01 \text{ g HF}}{1 \text{ mol HF}} = 43.57 \text{ g HF}$$

$$= 44 \text{ g HF (2 sig fig)}$$

The limiting reagent is H_2SO_4. Therefore, 23 g HF is the theoretical yield.

3. Calculate percent yield.

$$\% \text{ yield} = \frac{15 \text{ g HF}}{23 \text{ g HF}} \times 100\% = 65\%$$

This reaction is 65% efficient.

This procedure also works for calculating percent yield of a gas at STP.

CHECK YOUR KNOWLEDGE

1. What is stoichiometry?

2. How many grams of oxygen gas are needed to produce 87.5 g water, given the following unbalanced chemical reaction: $H_2 + O_2 \rightarrow H_2O$?

3. How many liters of sulfur dioxide gas are needed to react with 2.52 g O_2 gas at STP, given the following equation: $2SO_{2(g)} + O_{2(g)} \rightarrow 2SO_{3(g)}$?

4. What is a limiting reagent?

5. Calculate the mass of MgO produced if 1.80 g of Mg reacts with 12.25 g O_2 gas according to the following equation: $2Mg + O_2 \rightarrow 2MgO$. (Hint: You must calculate the limiting reagent first.)

6. 2.75 g of HCl are mixed with 12.00 g of $CaCO_3$, according to the balanced equation shown below. Calculate the theoretical yield of CO_2.

$2HCl + CaCO_3 \rightarrow CaCl_2 + H_2O + CO_2$

ANSWERS

CHECK YOUR ANSWERS

1. Stoichiometry is the quantitative study of the reactants and products in a reaction.

2. $\dfrac{87.5 \text{ g } H_2O}{1} \times \dfrac{1 \text{ mol } H_2O}{18.016 \text{ g } H_2O} \times \dfrac{1 \text{ mol } O_2}{2 \text{ mol } H_2O} \times \dfrac{32.00 \text{ g } O_2}{1 \text{ mol } O_2}$

= 77.7 g O_2

3. $\dfrac{2.52 \text{ g } O_2}{1} \times \dfrac{1 \text{ mol } O_2}{32.00 \text{ g } O_2} \times \dfrac{2 \text{ mol } SO_2}{1 \text{ mol } O_2} \times \dfrac{22.4 \text{ L } SO_2}{1 \text{ mol } SO_2}$

= 3.53 L of sulfur dioxide gas

4. The reactant that is used up first in a chemical reaction is called the limiting reagent.

5. $\dfrac{1.80 \text{ g } Mg}{1} \times \dfrac{1 \text{ mol } Mg}{24.3 \text{ g } Mg} \times \dfrac{2 \text{ mol } MgO}{2 \text{ mol } Mg} \times \dfrac{40.3 \text{ g } MgO}{1 \text{ mol } MgO}$

= 2.99 g MgO

$\dfrac{12.25 \text{ g } O_2}{1} \times \dfrac{1 \text{ mol } O_2}{32.00 \text{ g } O_2} \times \dfrac{2 \text{ mol } MgO}{1 \text{ mol } O_2} \times \dfrac{40.3 \text{ g } MgO}{1 \text{ mol } MgO}$

= 30.9 g MgO. Since the limiting reagent is Mg, the

mass of MgO produced will be 2.99.

6. $\dfrac{2.75\ g\ HCl}{1} \times \dfrac{1\ mol\ HCl}{36.46\ g\ HCl} \times \dfrac{1\ mol\ CO_2}{2\ mol\ HCl} \times \dfrac{44.01\ g\ CO_2}{1\ mol\ CO_2}$

$= 1.66\ g\ CO_2$

$\dfrac{12.00\ g\ CaCO_3}{1} \times \dfrac{1\ mol\ CaCO_3}{100.09\ g\ CaCO_3} \times \dfrac{1\ mol\ CO_2}{1\ mol\ CaCO_3} \times$

$\dfrac{44.01g\ CO_2}{1\ mol\ CO_2} = 5.28\ g\ CO_2$. Since the limiting reagent is HCl,

the theoretical yield to CO_2 is 1.66 g.

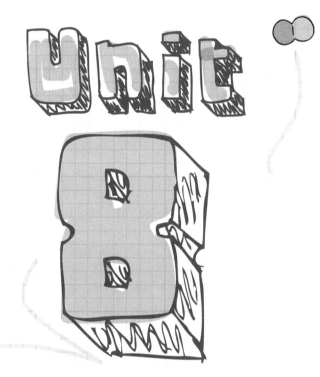

Unit 8

Gases

Chapter 22
COMMON GASES

IDENTIFYING COMMON GASES

You can identify some gases by the way they respond to certain stimuli.

Hydrogen: a wooden splint lit with a match at the end will make a popping sound when put into a test tube of hydrogen gas. A glowing splint will also burst into flame and relight.

Oxygen: a glowing wooden splint (smoldering when placed into a test tube of oxygen gas) will relight.

Carbon dioxide: a glowing wooden splint placed into a test tube of carbon dioxide gas will completely go out. Carbon dioxide gas also reacts in limewater to form a cloudy precipitate.

Ammonia: has a biting smell that might make your eyes water. It also turns red LITMUS PAPER blue.

Gases are one of the three main phases of matter (solid, liquid, gas). Unlike solids and liquids, the molecules in a gas are spread far apart. Because of their weak intermolecular forces, the gas molecules move independently of each other. (They bounce all over the place.)

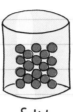  

Solid   Liquid   Gas

Gases are mostly found on the far-right side of the periodic table.

TYPES OF GASES

Group 18, the noble gases, exist as **MONOATOMIC** gases, a single atom that is not bonded to anything else.

Helium (He), oxygen (O), and hydrogen (H) are monoatomic gases.

The other elements exist as **DIATOMIC** gases, two atoms of the same element bonded together, such as O_2, H_2, and Cl_2.

Oxygen can also form ozone (O_3) when one monoatomic oxygen molecule (O) combines with a diatomic oxygen molecule (O_2).

Common Gases at Room Temperature

H_2 (hydrogen)	Ar (argon)
He (helium)	CO_2 (carbon dioxide)
CH_4 (methane)	N_2O (dinitrogen oxide)
NH_3 (ammonia)	C_3H_8 (propane)
Ne (neon)	NO_2 (nitrogen dioxide)
HCN (hydrogen cyanide)	O_3 (ozone)
CO (carbon monoxide)	C_4H_{10} (butane)
N_2 (nitrogen)	SO_2 (sulfur dioxide)
NO (nitrogen oxide)	BF_3 (boron trifluoride)
C_2H_6 (ethane)	Cl_2 (chlorine)
O_2 (oxygen)	Kr (krypton)
PH_3 (phosphine)	CF_2Cl_2 (dichlorodifluoromethane)
H_2S (hydrogen sulfide)	SF_6 (sulfur hexafluoride)
HCl (hydrogen chloride)	Xe (xenon)
F_2 (fluorine)	

UNITS OF MEASUREMENT FOR GASES

Gas molecules are in constant motion. They exert a force on everything they come into contact with, even other gases.

Gas can be measured in different ways. The common units used in gas measurements and calculations include:

Volume: in liters (L)

Temperature: in Kelvin (K)

Amount: in moles (mol)

Pressure: in atmospheres (atm) (other units are also used to measure pressure)

PRESSURE is dependent on *both* the force being exerted and the size of the area to which the force is applied.

PRESSURE
The force per unit area.

Formula for pressure:

$$P = \frac{force}{area} = \frac{F}{A}$$

The SI unit for pressure is Newtons per square meter (N/m^2), but these other units can also be used:

pascal   meters squared

$1 \text{ Pa} = 1 \text{ N/m}^2$ $1 \text{ atm} = 101.325 \text{ kPa}$ $1 \text{ kPa} = 1,000 \text{ Pa}$

Newton   atmosphere   kilopascal

Atmospheric Pressure

All gases that are found on Earth feel its gravitational pull. The air closest to Earth is denser than the air at higher altitudes. That is the reason why airplanes are pressurized. The air that is at the altitude at which a plane flies is too thin to breathe.

As you ascend into higher altitudes, the oxygen is thinner, and it is difficult to breathe. The cabin in a plane must be pressurized to the same level of atmospheric pressure that's on the ground so passengers can breathe without needing additional oxygen.

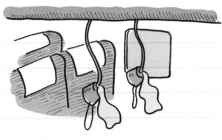

In the event of a loss of cabin pressure, pull the oxygen mask toward you and place over your nose and mouth.

The denser the atmosphere, the greater the pressure that it exerts. Scientists use **STANDARD ATMOSPHERIC PRESSURE**, the pressure at sea level, to keep measurements all the same so they can be compared.

STANDARD ATMOSPHERIC PRESSURE
1.00 atmospheres (atm) **or** 1.013×10^5 Pa **or** 101 kPa **or** 760 mmHg or Torr

A BAROMETER is the instrument used to measure atmospheric pressure.

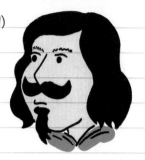

EVANGELISTA TORRICELLI (1608–1647) was the Italian physicist and mathematician who invented the barometer. His name is used today as one of the units, the Torr, to read the barometer.

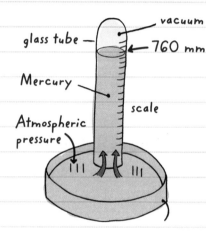

vacuum

glass tube

← 760 mm

Mercury

scale

Atmospheric pressure

Standard atmospheric pressure is equal to the pressure that supports a column of mercury (Hg) exactly 760.0 mm high at 0°C at sea level.

Sometimes you need to convert from one unit of measure for pressure to another.

FOR EXAMPLE: Convert 645 mmHg to atmospheres and kPa.

$$645 \text{ mmHg} \times \frac{1 \text{ atm}}{760 \text{ mmHg}} = .849 \text{ atm}$$

millimeters of mercury

$$645 \text{ mmHg} \times \frac{101 \text{ kPa}}{760 \text{ mmHg}} = 85.7 \text{ kPa}$$

CHECK YOUR KNOWLEDGE

1. How is a gas different from a solid or liquid?

2. If you place a glowing splint into a test tube of gas and it goes out, what type of gas is in the test tube?

3. Where on the periodic table are most gases found?

4. What is the difference between a monoatomic and a diatomic gas?

5. What are the four ways that a gas can be measured?

6. What is the equation for pressure?

7. What is standard atmospheric pressure? Name two different units that can be used to express it.

8. Convert 98,500 Pa to atmospheres.

ANSWERS

CHECK YOUR ANSWERS

1. Gases are less dense, have molecules that are farther apart, and are in constant motion.

2. Carbon dioxide

3. Gases are found in group 18 (noble gases), and some are in the nonmetal and halogen groups.

4. A monoatomic gas is composed of just one atom. A diatomic gas occurs when two atoms of the same element are bonded together.

5. Gases can be measured by volume in liters (L), temperature in Kelvin (K), amount in moles (mol), and pressure in atmospheres (atm).

6. Pressure is force per unit area. $P = F/A$.

7. Standard atmospheric pressure is the pressure at sea level and 0°C. The units that are used to express it are 1 atmosphere **OR** 1.013×10^5 Pa **or** 101 kPa **OR** 760 mmHg.

8. $98,500 \text{ Pa} \times \dfrac{1 \text{ atm}}{1.013 \times 10^5 \text{ Pa}} = .972 \text{ atm}$

Chapter 23

KINETIC MOLECULAR THEORY

HOW GASES BEHAVE

KINETIC MOLECULAR THEORY explains how ideal gases behave.

> ### KINETIC MOLECULAR THEORY OF GASES
> Theory that a gas consists of molecules in constant random motion.

Principles that comprise Kinetic Molecular Theory (ideal gases)

1. Gases are made of particles that remain in a state of constant random motion.

2. Gas particles do not have any attraction or repulsion (intermolecular forces) and will move continuously in a straight line until they collide with either another particle or the side of the container holding them.

3. Gas particles are extremely small—smaller than the spaces between them—which is why a gas is mostly empty space.

4. The average **KINETIC ENERGY** of the gas depends on the temperature of the gas and nothing else.

5. Collisions between particles are **ELASTIC**; they do not transfer energy from one particle to another, and no energy is lost.

Kinetic energy is the energy of movement.

If you are running, you are using kinetic energy.

POTENTIAL ENERGY is the stored energy that an object has because of its position relative to other objects.

If you are sitting in a chair, you have potential energy. The chair is holding you off the floor, and you could possibly fall off of it. Your energy is stored because of your position. The act of falling off the chair is kinetic energy.

Gas particles are in constant motion; therefore, they have high kinetic energy.

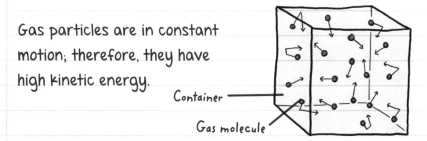

Container

Gas molecule

Collision of Gas Particles

Temperature directly affects kinetic energy.

As temperature increases, gas particles move more quickly. As temperature decreases, the gas particles slow down.

temperature ⬆ and kinetic energy ⬆
temperature ⬇ and kinetic energy ⬇

The more kinetic energy a gas has, the more collisions its particles will have. If the kinetic energy is high, the particles will be moving around a lot, resulting in more collisions. As the kinetic energy decreases, the number of collisions decreases.

Formula for determining the level of kinetic energy (KE)

$$KE = \frac{1}{2}mv^2$$

m = mass   v = velocity

The greater the number (n) of gas molecules, the greater the number of collisions.

It's like if you are in a swimming pool with three people—you will be able to avoid one another. If another fifty kids enter the pool, you'll be bumping into kids much more often.

CHECK YOUR KNOWLEDGE

1. What is the kinetic molecular theory of a gas?

2. True or false: The average kinetic energy of a gas depends on the temperature and nothing else.

3. True or false: Collisions between particles are completely inelastic, meaning that they do transfer energy from one particle to another and no energy is lost.

4. What is the difference between kinetic energy and potential energy?

5. What happens to the molecules of a gas when its kinetic energy is increased?

6. Under what conditions does the ideal gas law work best? When does it not work as well?

ANSWERS

CHECK YOUR ANSWERS

1. Gases constantly move in straight-line motion, with very small particles at large distances away from one another. They have no intermolecular forces of attraction.

2. True

3. False

4. Kinetic energy is the energy of movement. Potential energy is the energy that an object has because of its relative position to other objects.

5. The amount of collisions increases between the molecules themselves and with the container.

6. The ideal gas law is fairly accurate in that it provides values that are typically within 5% of the actual real-life values of the gas, under STP. It does not work well when the pressure of the gas is very high or the temperature is very low.

Chapter 24

GAS LAWS

GAS LAWS are mathematical rules about how a gas will behave under certain conditions.

BOYLE'S LAW

Boyle's law describes the relationship between pressure and volume.

Boyle's Law is named after 17th-century British chemist ROBERT BOYLE, who first suggested the relationship between pressure and volume of a gas.

> **Boyle's Law:** The pressure of a fixed amount of gas (p) at a constant temperature (t) is inversely proportional to the volume of the gas (V).
>
> $$P_1V_1 = P_2V_2$$

$P \sim \dfrac{1}{V}$, assuming that temperature and amount of gas remain the same.

As the pressure on a gas ⬆, the volume of the gas ⬇.
As the pressure on a gas ⬇, the volume of the gas ⬆.

Boyle's Law equation shows how the initial pressure (P_1) and volume (V_1) of a gas are equal to the final pressure (P_2) and volume (V_2) of a gas.

$$P_1V_1 = P_2V_2$$

Boyle's Law is only true if the number (n) of molecules and temperature (T) are kept the same.

Graph of Boyle's Law:

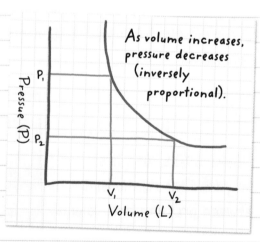

As volume increases, pressure decreases (inversely proportional).

FOR EXAMPLE: A sample of gas has a volume of 15.25 mL at 4.25 atm pressure. What will be the pressure if the volume is increased to 22.0 mL at a fixed temperature and amount of gas?

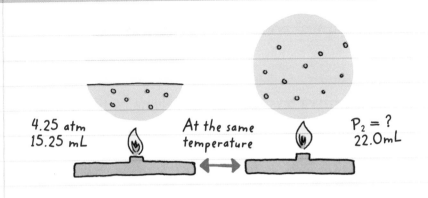

$$P_2 = \frac{P_1 \times V_1}{V_2} = \frac{(4.25 \text{ atm}) \times (15.25 \text{ mL})}{22.0 \text{ mL}} = 2.95 \text{ atm}$$

New pressure (P_2) = 2.95 atm

CHECK: Because the volume increased, the pressure should decrease.

CHARLES' LAW

JACQUES CHARLES was an 18th-century French physicist and the first to study the effect of temperature on the volume of a gas. Through experiments, he determined that volume and temperature are directly proportional to each other.

Charles' Law: The volume of a fixed amount of gas at a constant pressure is directly proportional to the absolute temperature of the gas.

Absolute temperature must be recorded in Kelvin (K).

$V \sim T$, assuming that pressure and amount of gas remain the same.

As the temperature on a gas ⬆, the volume of the gas ⬆.
As the temperature on a gas ⬇, the volume of the gas ⬇.

Charles' Law shows how the initial temperature (T_1) and volume (V_1) of a gas are proportional to the final temperature (T_2) and volume (V_2) of a gas.

$$\frac{V_1}{T_1} = \frac{V_2}{T_2}$$

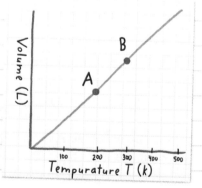

Graph of Charles' Law

As the temperature increases the volume increases.
A = 200K, 400L
B = 300K, 600L

Absolute temperature is always written in Kelvin (K) and has no negative values. To convert from Celsius to Kelvin, use the formula °C + 273 = K.

GAY-LUSSAC'S LAW

JOSEPH GAY-LUSSAC was an 18th-century French physicist and the first person to study the effect of temperature on the pressure of a gas. Through experiments, he determined that pressure and temperature are directly proportional to each other.

> **Gay-Lussac's Law:** The pressure of a fixed amount of gas at a constant volume is directly proportional to the absolute temperature of the gas.

$P \sim T$, assuming that volume and amount of gas remain the same.

> As the temperature on a gas ⬆, the pressure of the gas ⬆.
> As the temperature on a gas ⬇, the pressure of the gas ⬇.

Gay-Lussac's Law equation shows how the initial temperature (T_1) and pressure (P_1) of a gas are proportional to the final temperature (T_2) and pressure (P_2) of the gas.

$$\frac{P_1}{T_1} = \frac{P_2}{T_2}$$

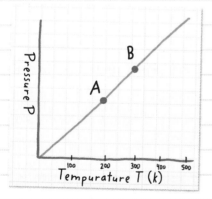

Graph of Gay-Lussac's Law

As the temperature increases, pressure increases.

COMBINED GAS LAW

The combined gas law puts the Boyle, Charles, and Gay-Lussac laws together and is used when temperature, pressure, and volume may all change.

COMBINED GAS LAW
Boyle + Charles + Gay-Lussac

What's important to remember about the combined gas law is that the amount of gas (moles) stays the same.

The formula for the combined gas law is

$$\frac{P_1 V_1}{T_1} = \frac{P_2 V_2}{T_2}$$

FOR EXAMPLE: 3.25 L of a gas at 40°C and 0.781 atm is brought to standard temperature and pressure (STP).

What will be the new gas volume?

1. Identify what you know (convert to Kelvin).

Known:

P_1 = .781 atm

T_1 = 40°C + 273 = 313 K

V_1 = 3.25 L

P_2 = 1.00 atm

T_2 = 273 K

V_2 = ?

> STP is 1 atm at 0°C
> (or 273 K)

2. Solve for missing information using the combined gas equation.

$$V_2 = \frac{T_2\, P_1\, V_1}{T_1\, P_2} = \frac{(273\text{ K})\,(.781\text{ atm})\,3.25\text{ L}}{(313\text{ K})\,(1.00\text{ atm})} = 2.21\text{ L}$$

CHECK: Because the temperature decreased and the pressure increased, the volume should decrease.

←

FOR EXAMPLE: The volume of a container is increased from 50.0 to 625 mL, which causes the pressure of the gas to increase from 700 to 1,250 mmHg. If the initial temperature was 65°C, what is the final temperature of the gas?

Known:

P_1 = 700 mmHg/760 mmHg = .92 atm
T_1 = 65°C + 273 = 338 K
V_1 = 50.0 mL/1,000 = .05 L
P_2 = 1250 mmHg/760 mmHg = 1.64 atm
T_2 = ?
V_2 = 625 mL/1,000 = .625 L

Solve for T_2:

$$T_2 = \frac{T_1\, P_2\, V_2}{V_1\, P_1} = \frac{(338\ K)\,(1.64\ atm)\,.625\ L}{(.050\ L)\,(.92\ atm)} = 7531 = 7500\ \text{(with}$$
2 sig figs) K

AVOGADRO'S LAW

Italian scientist AMEDEO AVOGADRO, the same person who is credited for coming up with Avogadro's number, determined that the volume of gases (V) at the same temperature and pressure contains the same number (n) of molecules.

> **Avogadro's Law:** At constant temperature and pressure, the volume of a gas is directly proportional to the number of moles of the gas.

$n \sim V$, assuming that temperature and pressure of the gas remain the same.

As the amount of gas ⬆, then volume of the gas ⬆.
As the amount of gas ⬇, then volume of the gas ⬇.

Avogadro's Law shows how the initial volume (V_1) and amount (n_1) of gas are proportional to the final volume (V_2) and amount (n_2) of gas.

$$\frac{V_1}{n_1} = \frac{V_2}{n_2} \text{ OR } V_1 n_2 = V_2 n_1$$

IDEAL GAS LAW

The IDEAL GAS LAW is a combination of Boyle's Law,
Charles' Law, Gay-Lussac's Law, and Avogadro's Law.

IDEAL GAS LAW
Boyle + Charles + Gay-Lussac + Avogadro

The ideal gas law describes the relationship among
pressure (P), volume (V), temperature (T), and the amount (n)
of gas. It explains what would happen for an ideal gas,
with three assumptions:

- The gas particles have no forces acting among them (meaning they don't feel attraction or repulsion forces).

- The gas particles do not take up any space, because their atomic volume is completely ignored.

- The behavior of the gases follows Kinetic Molecular Theory.

The ideal gas equation is fairly accurate for most ranges of temperature and pressure. For more accurate readings for conditions of high pressure and low temperature, use Van der Waals equation.

The ideal gas law: $PV = nRT$

P = pressure
V = volume (must be in liters)
n = amount of gas in moles

R = gas constant
T = temperature (must be in Kelvin)

R is a universal constant that relates energy and temperature. Because energy can be defined as pressure × volume, R is used to quantify the relationship between temperature and amount of gas.

Solving for the universal gas constant (R) using 1 mol of gas at standard temperature and pressure, the value of R will change depending on the pressure value and unit.

Calculation using atmospheres:

If you assume that the gas is at STP, then you can solve for R.

$$R = \frac{PV}{nT} = \frac{(1.00 \text{ atm}) (22.4 \text{ L})}{(1.00 \text{ mol}) (273 \text{ K})} = .0821 \text{ L atm/mol K}$$

R can be represented with any of the following units:

$R = 0.0821$ L atm/mol K (most commonly used)
$R = 8.3145$ J/mol K
$R = 8.2057$ m³ atm/mol K
$R = 62.3637$ L Torr/mol K or L mmHg/mol K

FOR EXAMPLE: A sample of nitrogen gas is kept in a container with a volume of 3.3 L and a temperature of 34°C. A pressure of 5.6 atm is exerted on the gas. How many moles of the gas are present?

1. Identify what you know.

$T = 34°C + 273 = 307 \text{ K}$

$P = 5.6 \text{ atm}$

$V = 3.3 \text{ L}$

$R = 0.0821 \text{ L atm/mol K}$

2. Solve for n.

$$n = \frac{PV}{RT} = \frac{(5.6 \text{ atm})(3.3 \text{ L})}{(0.0821)(307 \text{ K})} = .73 \text{ mol present}$$

USING THE IDEAL GAS LAW TO FIND DENSITY AND MOLAR MASS

You can move around the parts of the formula for the ideal gas law to determine density and molar mass, assuming that you maintain the original relationships.

$$PV = nRT$$

For example: Density = mass/volume, although volume is in the ideal gas law, while mass is not.

Solution: n, the number of moles of a gas, is determined by dividing the mass (m) of the gas by its molar mass (M):

$$n = \frac{m}{M}$$

If you replace n with the above, you get $PV = \left(\frac{m}{M}\right) * RT$.

If you use $d = \frac{m}{V}$, then you can rearrange the equation to $P = \frac{mRT}{(MV)}$.

To include density (d):

$$\underset{\text{density}}{\longrightarrow} d = \frac{m}{V} = \frac{PM}{RT}$$

pressure — molar mass — gas constant — temperature

DALTON'S LAW OF PARTIAL PRESSURE

JOHN DALTON was an English scientist known as a pioneer of modern atomic theory. To determine the relationship of pressure, temperature, volume, and amount in a mixture of gases, use a law based on Dalton's experimental work.

Dalton's **Law of Partial Pressure** states that the total pressure of a mixture of gases is the sum of the pressures of each individual gas.

If you have two different gases represented by A and B, the total pressure is equal to the sum of their pressures.

$$P_{TOTAL} = P_A + P_B$$

FOR EXAMPLE: A cylinder of compressed natural gas has a volume of 19.0 L and contains 1213 g of methane (CH_4) and 238 g of ethane (C_2H_6). The temperature is 28.0°C. Determine the total pressure in the cylinder and the partial pressure of each gas.

1. Calculate the moles of each gas using the periodic table.

Mol CH_4 = 1213 g × $\dfrac{1 \text{ mol } CH_4}{16.05 \text{ g}}$ = 75.58 mol

Mol C_2H_6 = 238 g × $\dfrac{1 \text{ mol } C_2H_6}{30.03 \text{ g}}$ = 7.93 mol

2. Determine the pressure of each gas individually using the ideal gas law.

$P_{methane} = \dfrac{nRT}{V} = \dfrac{(75.58 \text{ mol})(.0821 \text{ L atm/mol K})(28+273 \text{ K})}{19.0 \text{ L}}$

= 98.3 atm

$$P_{ETHANE} = \frac{nRT}{V} = \frac{(7.93 \text{ mol}) (.0821 \text{ L atm/mol K}) (28 + 273 \text{ K})}{19.0 \text{ L}}$$

$$= 10.3 \text{ atm}$$

3. Add the pressure of each gas.

$P_{TOTAL} = P_{METHANE} + P_{ETHANE}$
$\qquad = 98.3 \text{ atm} + 10.3 \text{ atm} = 108.6 \text{ atm}$

AIR IS A MIXTURE OF MANY DIFFERENT GASES: 78% NITROGEN, 21% OXYGEN, AND 1% OTHER GASES.

CHECK YOUR KNOWLEDGE

1. What are the gas laws and why are they important?

2. Which gas law shows the relationship between volume and temperature?

3. What is the ideal gas law and why is it important? Provide the equation itself.

4. Why do we apply Dalton's Law of Partial Pressure?

5. 7.15 L of a gas is at 1.86 atm. What pressure is obtained when the volume is changed to 12.3 L?

ANSWERS ➡ 345

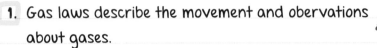

1. Gas laws describe the movement and obervations about gases.

2. Charles's Law shows the relationship between volume and temperature.

3. The ideal gas equation is a combination of Boyle's Law, Charles's Law, Gay-Lussac's Law, and Avogadro's Law. It is important to be able to make adjustments to every aspect of experiments: pressure, temperature, volume, and amount (moles) of the gas. $PV = nRT$.

4. Dalton's Law of Partial Pressure allows for the total relationship of pressure, temperature, volume, and amount of mixed gases to be determined.

5. $(7.15)(1.86)/(12.3) = 1.08$ atm

Unit 9

Solutions and Solubility

Chapter 25

SOLUBILITY

SOLUBLE VS INSOLUBLE

A mixture is a substance made by combining elements or compounds in a way that doesn't produce a chemical reaction. There are two kinds of mixtures: **HOMOGENEOUS** and **HETEROGENEOUS**.

Homo is Greek for "same." →

Homogeneous mixtures are uniform (evenly mixed) throughout, and components are evenly distributed. This type of mixture cannot be separated by physical means such as filtration, evaporation, or decanting.

Sometimes, homogeneous mixtures are called **SOLUTIONS**.

Examples: seawater, lemonade

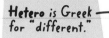

Heterogeneous mixtures are made up
of substances that are not evenly mixed
and can be separated by physical means.

Examples: pizza, fruit salad, and oil
and water

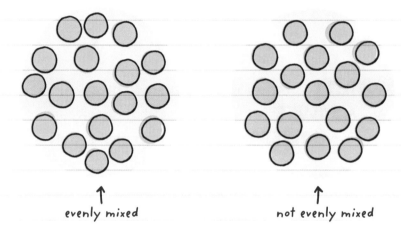

↑
evenly mixed

↑
not evenly mixed

When two substances combine within a solution, they
can be either **SOLUBLE** or **INSOLUBLE**. A substance
that is soluble will completely dissolve in the solution.
An insoluble substance does not completely dissolve in
the solution.

Things to know!

SOLUBILITY is the ability of a solute to dissolve in a solvent. A **SOLUTE** is the substance that dissolves in a solution. A **SOLVENT** is the substance that dissolves.

For example: If you add a tablespoon of chocolate powder to a glass of milk and stir:

The milk is the **solvent**.

The chocolate powder is the **solute**.

The chocolate milk is the **solution**.

That solution did not produce a precipitate, because the chocolate powder was *soluble* in the milk; it completely dissolved.

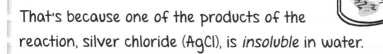
SOLUBILITY ON A MOLECULAR LEVEL

Water is a clear, colorless liquid. If you could examine
it at the molecular level, you would see a group of water
molecules floating around. The water molecules may move
about and bump into each other or remain bonded together.

If some table sugar (sucrose, $C_{12}H_{22}O_{11}$) is added to the water, the
molecules of sucrose start moving among the water molecules.

The sugar is the **solute**.

The water is the **solvent**.

Molecules of water surround
the sugar molecules.

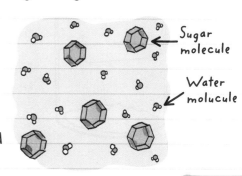
Sugar molecule

Water molucule

The molecules within the solid sucrose molecule start to move about and break apart. This movement is called **RANDOM MOLECULAR MOTION**. As the sucrose molecules separate from each other, they spread out and begin to dissolve in the water. As the sucrose molecules become increasingly separated from each other, random molecular motion continues to separate them among the solvent (water) molecules, speeding up the dissolving process.

The faster the sucrose molecules move apart, the faster the dissolving process.

RANDOM MOLECULAR MOTION
The unpredictable movement and breaking apart of molecules or atoms within a solution.

The process will look like this:

Water

Sugar
solution

Sugar

TYPES OF SOLUTIONS

In a solution, the solute and solvent are not chemically bonded to each other.

Solutions can be a mix of

- gas-gas
- liquid-liquid
- solid-solid
- or any combination of gas, liquid, or solid

FOR EXAMPLE: Salt (NaCl) mixes with water (H_2O) in the ocean. Identify the solute, solvent, and type of solution.

Answer: Because the concentration of water in the ocean is much higher than the concentration of salt, salt is the solute. Water is the solvent, and the salt water is a liquid-solid mixture.

- With iced tea mix and water, identify the solute, solvent, and type of solution.

Answer: There is much more water than iced tea mix, so the water is the solvent and the iced tea mix is the solute. The mixture is a liquid-solid solution.

FOR EXAMPLE: Carbon dioxide (CO_2) is mixed into cola to form soda. Identify the solute, solvent, and type of solution.

Answer: Because there is more cola than carbon dioxide, CO_2 is the solute, cola is the solvent, and the carbonated soda is a gas-liquid solution.

Solutions are classified into three main types:
- **SATURATED**
- **UNSATURATED**
- **SUPERSATURATED**

A saturated solution contains the maximum amount of solute possible. If you add any more solute, it will settle at the bottom of the solution because it cannot dissolve.

An unsaturated solution contains less than the maximum amount of solute possible. You could add more solute, and it would dissolve.

A supersaturated solution holds more solute than is normally possible in a saturated solution. This happens when the solution is heated to a high temperature, more solute is added to saturate the hot solution, and then the solution is cooled quickly without forming a precipitate.

COLLOIDS AND SUSPENSIONS

A **COLLOID** is a homogeneous solution that is made up of larger particles but the substance remains evenly distributed throughout.

COLLOID
Combination of two substances, where the molecules of one substance are much larger than those of the other substance but they are still evenly distributed throughout.

Water is made up of hydrogen and oxygen ions dissolved in the water. It is homogeneous, but not a colloid. Particles of milk are much larger than the hydrogen and oxygen molecules of water. Milk is a colloid. It is made up of about 87% water and 13% other solids, such as fat, proteins, lactose, and minerals. Just like water, milk is a homogeneous mixture; it is the same throughout.

There are four types of colloids:

SOL is a colloidal suspension with solid particles in a liquid.

mixture that looks uniform when stirred or shaken but separates into different layers when allowed to settle

Muddy water: Mud contains larger particles that are partially dissolved in the water.

EMULSION is a colloidal suspension that is formed between two liquids.

Oil and vinegar salad dressing

FOAM is a colloidal suspension that is formed when multiple gas particles are trapped in a liquid or solid.

Foam soap

AEROSOL is a colloidal suspension containing small solid or liquid particles that are evenly spread throughout a gas.

Spray can

SUSPENSIONS form after mixing:

liquid + liquid
solid + liquid
liquid + gas

In a suspension, the two substances are combined physically, not chemically. They need an outside force to get them to mix, such as stirring or shaking. When they are allowed to sit for a while and settle, the two substances will separate again.

One of the most common suspensions is oil and vinegar (salad dressing). Other common suspensions include sand in water or dust/droplets of oil in air.

Oil-and-vinegar suspension: The larger particles are the oil, and the smaller particles are the vinegar. As the two substances separate, the oil will form on top because it is less dense (lighter).

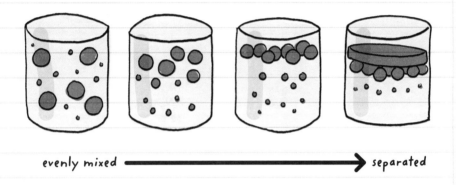

evenly mixed ⟶ separated

CHECK YOUR KNOWLEDGE

1. What is the difference between a substance that is soluble and one that is insoluble?

2. A solution contains less than the maximum amount of solute possible. What type of solution is it?

3. A solution is heated to a high temperature with added solute, and then cooled quickly without forming a precipitate. What type of solution is it?

4. What is a colloid?

5. Are solutions a result of a physical or chemical change?

6. What is the difference between a foam and an aerosol?

7. Define the term *suspension* and give an example of a suspension.

ANSWERS

CHECK YOUR ANSWERS

1. A substance that is soluble will completely dissolve in the solution. An insoluble substance is one that does not dissolve in the solution.

2. An unsaturated solution

3. A supersaturated solution

4. A colloid is a homogeneous solution that is composed of larger particles but is still the same substance throughout.

5. Solutions are a result of physical changes.

6. Foam is created when multiple gas particles are trapped in a liquid or solid. An aerosol contains small solid or liquid particles that are spread evenly throughout the gas.

7. Suspensions are heterogeneous mixtures that have solid particles in a fluid. Suspensions form from mixing two liquids, a solid and a liquid or gas, or a liquid and a gas. In a suspension, the two substances are combined physically, not chemically. Example: salad dressing.

Chapter 26

SOLUBILITY RULES AND CONDITIONS

SOLUBILITY AND IONIC COMPOUNDS

Aqueous solvents are great for dissolving ionic compounds. The water causes the ionic crystal bonds to separate and split up into their original ions. This process is called **DISSOCIATION OF IONS**. The polar ends of the water molecule have a strong pull on the positive and negative ions within the crystal, causing them to break apart.

This equation describes a dissociation reaction (shows what happens when a salt molecule [NaCl] dissociates in water):

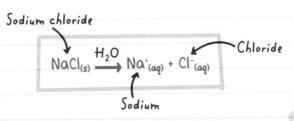

Sodium chloride

Chloride

$$NaCl_{(s)} \xrightarrow{H_2O} Na^+_{(aq)} + Cl^-_{(aq)}$$

Sodium

PRECIPITATION REACTIONS are one of the most common types of chemical reactions that occur in an aqueous solution. During a precipitation reaction, an insoluble solid, called a precipitate, is formed.

Sometimes, ions are not involved in the formation of a precipitate. These ions are called **SPECTATOR IONS**. When spectator ions are present, write an equation that shows only the ions taking part in the reaction. Ignore the spectator ions.

This type of equation is called a **NET IONIC EQUATION**.

A **net ionic equation** does not include spectator ions. It only shows the ions that are taking part in the reaction.

Rules for writing ionic and net ionic equations:

1. Write a balanced equation for the reaction.

2. Use the solubility table to determine whether a precipitate will form. Label all reactants and products with (aq) if soluble or (s) if insoluble, based on the solubility rules.

3. Write the ionic equation for the reaction. Dissociate all reactants and products labeled (aq). Do not dissociate any reactants or products labeled (s).

4. Identify and cancel out the spectator ions.

5. Rewrite the final equation as a "net ionic equation" without the spectator ions.

Make sure the total charge to the left of the arrow equals the total charge to the right of the arrow.

For the reaction:

$$AgNO_{3\,(aq)} + NaCl_{(aq)} \rightarrow AgCl_{(s)} + NaNO_{3\,(aq)}$$

$$Ag^+ + \cancel{NO_3^-} + \cancel{Na^+} + Cl^- \rightarrow AgCl + \cancel{Na^+} + \cancel{NO_3^-} \quad \text{cross out spectator ions}$$

The net ionic equation is:

$$Ag^+_{(aq)} + Cl^-_{(aq)} \rightarrow AgCl_{(s)}$$

The spectator ions nitrate and sodium did not affect the reaction.

> **Spectator ions** are ions that are not chemically changed over the course of a reaction. A net ionic equation includes only the ions that are chemically changed in the overall reaction.

SOLUBILITY RULES

Solubility rules help you to determine whether a substance is soluble or insoluble.

SOLUBILITY RULE	EXCEPTION
1. All alkali metals and ammonium salts are soluble.	None
2. All nitrates, chlorates, and perchlorates are soluble.	None
3. All silver, lead (II), and mercury (I) salts are insoluble.	$AgNO_3$ and $Ag(2H_3O_2)$ are common soluble salts of silver.
4. All chlorides, bromides, and iodides are soluble.	Except when combined with Ag^+, Pb^{2+}, and Hg^{2+}
5. All carbonates, oxides, sulfides, hyroxides, phosphates, chromates, and sulfites are insoluble.	Calcium sulfide, strontium sulfide, and barium hydroxide are soluble.
6. All sulfates are soluble.	Calcium sulfate, strontium sulfate, and barium hydroxate are insoluble.

FOR EXAMPLE: Both iron (III) nitrate $Fe(NO_3)_3$ and sodium hydroxide (NaOH) completely dissociate in water. What will be the net ionic equation if you mix iron (III) hydroxide and sodium nitrate in an aqueous solution?

1. Write the balanced equation.

$Fe(NO_3)_3 + 3NaOH \rightarrow Fe(OH)_3 + 3NaNO_3$

2. According to the solubility table, $Fe(OH)_3$ will form a precipitate. All other substances dissociate in an aqueous solution.

3. Write the ionic equation.

$Fe^{3+}_{(aq)} + 3NO_3^-_{(aq)} + 3Na^+_{(aq)} + 3OH^-_{(aq)} \rightarrow Fe(OH)_{3(s)} + 3NO_3^-_{(aq)} + 3Na^+_{(aq)}$

4. Identify and cancel out spectator ions.

$Fe^{3+}_{(aq)} + 3\cancel{NO_3^-_{(aq)}} + 3\cancel{Na^+_{(aq)}} + 3OH^-_{(aq)} \rightarrow Fe(OH)_{3(s)} + 3\cancel{NO_3^-_{(aq)}} + 3\cancel{Na^+_{(aq)}}$

5. Write the net ionic equation.

$Fe^{3+}_{(aq)} + 3OH^-_{(aq)} \rightarrow Fe(OH)_{3(s)}$

ELECTROLYTIC PROPERTIES

Solutes in an aqueous solution are classified as either **ELECTROLYTES** or **NONELECTROLYTES**.

An **electrolyte** is a substance that when dissolved in water will conduct electricity.

A **nonelectrolyte** is a substance that when dissolved in water will not conduct electricity.

You can use an ELECTRICAL CONDUCTIVITY TESTER to test for conductivity.

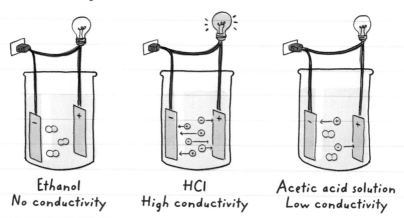

Ethanol	HCl	Acetic acid solution
No conductivity	High conductivity	Low conductivity

Each of the beakers above contains a solution and two electrical plates. One plate is positively charged, and the other is negatively charged. The plates are hooked to an electrical outlet and a light bulb. Once the charge runs to the plates, the positive ions are attracted to the negative plate, and the negative ions are attracted to the positive plate.

The beaker on the left is a NONELECTROLYTE. This means that none of the ions move toward the positively charged or negatively charged side.

The beaker on the right is a weak electrolyte, and the beaker in the middle is a strong electrolyte.

The more the ions in the solution move, the greater the presence of electrolytes and the greater the electrical charge created for the light bulb.

FACTORS THAT AFFECT SOLUBILITY

Temperature affects the rate of solubility in solids. When temperature increases, the particles in a solid move around faster. This makes solids dissolve more quickly and solubility increases.

When the temperature is reduced, particles of both the solute and solvent move more slowly and solubility decreases.

Gases respond to temperature in the opposite way. When the temperature increases, the gas also moves faster but it escapes the liquid phase and leaves the solution (solubility decreases). When the temperature decreases, solubility increases.

Pressure affects gases when mixed with liquids.
As pressure decreases, solubility of the gas decreases.
As pressure increases, solubility of the gas increases.

Gases can be dissolved in liquid, too!

⬆ Temperature ⬆ Solubility of solids

⬇ Temperature ⬇ Solubility of solids

⬆ Pressure ⬆ Solubility of gases in liquids

⬇ Pressure ⬇ Solubility of gases in liquids

Cola is created by increasing the pressure of carbon dioxide gas molecules so that they dissolve in the liquid cola. At normal pressure, the CO_2 particles convert to gas and will move out of the cola, causing it to go "flat."

CHECK YOUR KNOWLEDGE

1. What is dissociation of ions?

2. Why is water a good solvent for ionic compounds?

3. Most sulfate salts are soluble in water. Name three compounds that are the exception to this rule.

4. True or false: Salts containing group 1 ions are soluble in water.

5. What type of solutions are the following?
   A. Air
   B. Milk
   C. Salt water from the ocean

6. Write the net ionic equation for
   $ZnCl_2 + Na_2S \rightarrow ZnS + 2NaCl$.

7. What is the difference between an electrolyte and a nonelectrolyte?

8. How do pressure and temperature affect the solubility of a gas?

ANSWERS ⟩ 369

CHECK YOUR ANSWERS

1. Dissociation of ions occurs when water causes the ionic crystal bonds to separate and split up into their original ions.

2. The polar ends of the water molecule exert a force of attraction on the positive and negative ions within the crystal, thus causing them to break apart.

3. Sulfate salts that are insoluble in water include $CaSO_4$, $BaSO_4$, $PbSO_4$, Ag_2SO_4, and $SrSO_4$.

4. True: Salts containing group 1 ions are soluble in water.

5. **A.** Air is a mixture.
   B. Milk is a colloid.
   C. Ocean salt water is homogeneous.

6. The net ionic equation is $Zn^{2+}_{(aq)} + S^{2-}_{(aq)} \rightarrow ZnS_{(s)}$.

7. An electrolyte is a substance that when dissolved in water will conduct electricity. A nonelectrolyte is a substance that when dissolved in water will not conduct electricity.

8. A gas dissolved in liquid will have greater solubility at LOWER temperatures and HIGHER pressure. The energy of the gas molecules causes them to escape more easily, like soda left out on a hot summer day.

HEY, AREN'T THEY GOING TO JOIN US?

NO THEY'RE JUST SPECTATORS.

Chapter 27

CONCENTRATIONS OF SOLUTIONS

MIXING SOLUTIONS

When mixing a solution, you need to know

1. the amount of solute and solvent to use.

2. the **CONCENTRATION** of the solution.
The concentration tells the amount of solute
that is dissolved in the solvent.

Concentration can be calculated in different ways.

One way to calculate concentration is

Molarity (M) or mol/L $= \dfrac{\text{moles of solute}}{\text{Liters of solution}} = \dfrac{n}{V}$

This measure of concentration is most often used to prepare solutions for which the total volume of solution is known and accounted for.

To calculate moles of the solute, use the molar mass of the element or compound to convert from grams to moles.

FOR EXAMPLE: What is the molarity of a solution prepared with 45.6 g $NaNO_3$ and 250 mL water?

1. Convert the mass of $NaNO_3$ to mol $NaNO_3$.

$$45.6 \text{ g} \times \frac{1 \text{ mol } NaNO_3}{85.01 \text{ g } NaNO_3} = .536 \text{ mol}$$

2. Convert milliliters to liters.

$$250 \text{ mL} \times \frac{1 \text{ L}}{1,000 \text{ mL}} = .250 \text{ L}$$

3. Calculate molarity (M).

$$M = \frac{.536 \text{ mol}}{.250 \text{ L}} = 2.14 \text{ mol/L}$$

MOLALITY gives you the number of moles of solute dissolved in exactly 1 kg of solvent.

$$\text{Molality (m)} = \frac{\text{moles of solute}}{\text{mass of solvent in kg}} = \text{mol/kg}$$

MOLARITY vs MOLALITY

Molarity is the number of moles of a solute dissolved in a solution.
Molality is the number of moles of a solute dissolved in a solvent.

Molality is important when you are adding solute to a solvent in an experiment and figuring out the **COLLIGATIVE PROPERTIES** of the solution.

COLLIGATIVE PROPERTY
A physical property of a solution that depends on the ratio of the amount of solute to the solvent, *not the type of solvent.*

Molarity is TEMPERATURE DEPENDENT (when the temperature increases, the volume slightly increases as well).

Molality is not temperature dependent (there is no volume measurement in the calculation).

Salt increases water's boiling point. Salty water takes longer to boil.

When a solute (ice cream) is added to the solvent (cola), the freezing point goes down.

Molality is used when the MASS of SOLVENT (not the total solution's volume) must be known for a given calculation (such as colligative property formulas).

Colligative properties include:
freezing-point depression
boiling-point elevation
vapor-pressure reduction

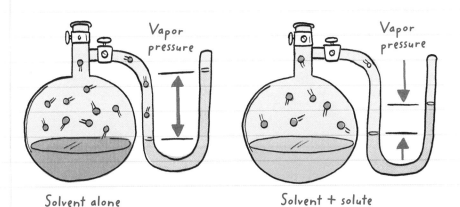

Solvent alone

Solvent + solute

When a solute is added to the solvent, then **vapor pressure** of the solvent reduces.

FOR EXAMPLE: Calculate the molality (M) of a calcium hydroxide solution that has 35.4 g of calcium hydroxide dissolved in 278 g of water.

1. Convert the mass of calcium hydroxide to moles.

$$35.4 \text{ g } Ca(OH)_2 \times \frac{1 \text{ mol } Ca(OH)_2}{74.09 \text{ g } Ca(OH)_2} = .478 \text{ mol } Ca(OH)_2$$

2. Convert grams of water to kilograms.

$$278 \text{ g} \times \frac{1 \text{ kg}}{1,000 \text{ g}} = 0.278 \text{ kg}$$

3. Calculate molality.

$$M = \frac{.478 \text{ mol } Ca(OH)_2}{.278 \text{ kg water}} = 1.72 \text{ mol/kg}$$

Percent Composition by Mass

If we assume that 1 mL of a water-based solution has a mass of 1 g, 1 L of the solution has a mass of 1,000 g, because the density of water is 1 g/1 mL.

$$\% \text{ composition by mass} = \frac{\text{mass of the solute}}{\text{mass of the solution}} \times 100$$

Parts per Million

This measure of concentration is most often used in very dilute solutions. Parts per million (ppm) describes the ratio parts of solute per 1 million units of solution.

$$\text{Parts per million (ppm)} = \frac{\text{units of solute}}{\text{one million units of solution}}$$

Solubility

This measure of concentration is sometimes the unit given in charts and tables or specified in the solubility rules.

$$\text{Solubility: grams/liter (g/L)} = \frac{\text{mass of the solute (in grams)}}{\text{volume of solvent (in liters)}}$$

DILUTIONS

Chemists sometimes need to dilute or reduce the concentration of their solutions. Dilution occurs when more solvent is added to a fixed amount of solute. The solution is mixed to ensure that the solvent is spread equally throughout.

A **VOLUMETRIC FLASK** is made to contain an exact volume at a specific temperature. Volumetric flasks, used for precise dilutions and preparation of standard solutions, have one line of measurement indicating the exact amount of volume contained.

250 ml

How do you know how much solvent to add?

Use the dilution formula:

$$M_1 V_1 = M_2 V_2$$

M_1: molarity of the stock or the more concentrated solution
M_2: the final or diluted concentration
V_1: the volume of the concentrated solution to be added
V_2: the total volume of diluted solution to be prepared
$M_1 V_1$: the molarity and volume of the solution *before* dilution
$M_2 V_2$: the molarity and volume of the solution *after* dilution

STOICHIOMETRY WITH SOLUTIONS

For volume stoichiometry, use molarity, NOT gas volume stoichiometry.

FOR EXAMPLE: A chemist dissolved 8.84 g of NaCl in water and then poured the solution into a 500 mL volume flask, adding enough water to make the solution exactly 350.00 mL. What is the concentration of the solution?

Look for molarity.

Start with the NaCl because that is what is placed into the water. Convert grams of NaCl to moles.

$$8.84 \text{ g NaCl} \times \frac{1 \text{ mol NaCl}}{58.45 \text{ g NaCl}} = .15 \text{ mol NaCl}$$

Divide the moles of NaCl by the amount of water in 350.00 mL.

.15 mol NaCl/.350 L = .429 M,
the concentration of the solution

FOR EXAMPLE: How many grams of potassium hydroxide (KOH) are contained in 32.0 mL of a solution whose concentration is 2.56 M?

Use molarity and formula mass.

$$.032 \text{ L KOH} \times \frac{2.56 \text{ M}}{1 \text{ L KOH}} = .082 \text{ mol} \times \frac{56.11 \text{ g}}{1 \text{ mol KOH}} = 4.60 \text{ g KOH}$$

CHECK YOUR KNOWLEDGE

1. What does concentration tell you?

2. Which measure of concentration is commonly used when creating solutions? How is it expressed?

3. What is molality and why is it important?

4. Define the term colligative property and give two examples.

5. A chemist dissolved 12.95 g of $MgSO_4$ in water and then poured the solution into a 750 mL volumetric flask, adding enough water to make the solution exactly 750.00 mL. What is the concentration of the solution?

6. Determine the amount of $CaCl_2$ (in grams) that is found in 45.5 mL of a solution with a concentration of 3.32 M.

ANSWERS ⟶ 381

CHECK YOUR ANSWERS

1. Concentration tells you the amount of solute that is dissolved in the solvent.

2. To prepare solutions, the molarity measure of concentration is most often used in both chemistry and biology. Molarity is measured in moles/liter.

3. Molality gives you the number of moles of solute dissolved in exactly 1 kg of solvent. Molarity is important when conducting an experiment when you are adding solute to a solvent and when determining colligative properties of the solution.

4. A colligative property is a physical property of a solution that depends only on the ratio of the amount of solute to the solvent, *not the type of solvent*. Colligative properties include freezing-point depression, boiling-point elevation, and vapor-pressure reduction.

5. The concentration of the described solution is 0.1434 M.

6. The amount of $CaCl_2$ is 16.8 g.

Unit 10

Acids and Bases

Chapter 28

PROPERTIES OF ACIDS AND BASES

ACID OR BASE?

The Swedish chemist SVANTE ARRHENIUS was first to classify **ACIDS** and **BASES**. When examining their properties in an aqueous solution, he found that:

Acids are substances that dissociate (separate) in water to produce hydrogen (H^+) ions.

Bases are substances that dissociate in water to produce hydroxide (OH^-) ions.

Svante Arrhenius (1859–1927), was awarded the Nobel Prize for Chemistry in 1903.

NEUTRALIZATION happens when an acid and base mix and the hydrogen ions and hydroxide ions combine to produce water. The anion and cation of the acid and base combine to form a salt.

NEUTRALIZATION
The formation of a salt and water.

BRONSTED-LOWRY ACIDS AND BASES

The Arrhenius definition of acids and bases only explained acids and bases that actually contained H^+ and OH^-. His definition was limited because it didn't explain everything found in water (like ammonia).

Danish chemist JOHANNES BRONSTED and English physicist THOMAS MARTIN LOWRY came up with a way to address the holes in the Arrhenius definition.

They created the BRONSTED-LOWRY THEORY, which defined acids and bases by their **ability to accept or donate a proton.**

Hydrogen (H⁺) is also called a proton because the H atom consists of only one proton and one electron, but the H⁺ ion lost its electron, and the only particle left is a proton.

A Bronsted-Lowry acid is a proton donor: It donates a H^+ ion to a Bronsted base.

A Bronsted-Lowry base is a proton acceptor: It accepts a H^+ ion from a Bronsted acid.

$$HCl_{(aq)} + NH_{3(aq)} \rightarrow NH_4^+{}_{(aq)} + Cl^-{}_{(aq)}$$

In this reaction, HCl donates a H^+ ion to ammonia (NH_3), so the HCl is an acid. NH_3 is the base because it accepts the H^+ ion from the acid to become NH_4^+.

Water can be considered a Bronsted base. In this reaction, $HCl + H_2O \rightarrow H_3O^+ + Cl^-$

Water can also be a Bronsted acid. In this reaction, $NH_3 + H_2O \rightarrow NH_4^+ + OH^-$

the HCl (hydrochloric acid) donates a proton to water to create H_3O^+, the hydronium ion. So, HCl is the acid and water is the base, because it accepts a proton.

> To remember these acid and base roles, use the following acronym:
>
> ### B A A D
> ### **B**ases **A**ccept; **A**cids **D**onate

PROPERTIES OF ACIDS AND BASES

Almost every liquid has properties of an acid or a base. Ways to tell an acid from a base:

Properties of acids

- a sour taste (never taste anything in the lab!)

- changes the color of litmus paper.
  Blue litmus will turn red, and red litmus will stay red.

- reacts with certain metals to produce hydrogen gas

- conducts electricity in an aqueous solution

- reacts with carbonates and bicarbonates to produce carbon dioxide gas

Properties of bases
- a bitter taste

- changes the color of litmus paper
  (Blue litmus stays blue; red litmus turns blue. Substances that are close to neutral will not change litmus color; red stays red and blue stays blue.)

- conducts electricity in an aqueous solution

- feels slippery

NEUTRALIZATION REACTIONS

When acids and bases react, they form salts. A salt is the combination of a cation (⁺) from the acid and an anion (⁻) from the base. When the two bond, they have a neutral (zero) charge.

NEUTRALIZATION REACTIONS
Reactions in which an acid and a base react to form a salt.

For example, in the reaction

$KOH + HCl \rightarrow KCl + H_2O$

KCl is the salt that is formed.

The dissociation reaction would be:

$K^+ + OH^- + H^+ + Cl^- \rightarrow K^+ + Cl^- + H_2O$

K and Cl are spectator ions and will cancel out, leaving only water.

Examples of neutralization reactions:

- Metal oxides and metal hydroxides:

  Acid + metal oxide (base) → salt + water

  Acid + metal hydroxide (base) → salt + water

- Carbonates and hydrogen carbonates:

Acid + metal carbonate → salt + water + carbon dioxide

Acid + metal hydrogen carbonate → salt + water + carbon dioxide

Your stomach contains hydrochloric acid (HCl), a very strong acid that helps to break down food. If you have indigestion (an upset stomach), you might take an antacid tablet. That tablet is made of magnesium hydroxide—a base. You are neutralizing excess stomach acid by adding a base.

CHECK YOUR KNOWLEDGE

1. What is an acid?

2. What is a base?

3. Under what circumstances does neutralization occur?

4. How can you tell an acid from a base using litmus paper?

5. What properties do acids and bases have in common?

6. What is a salt and how it is formed?

7. How did Bronsted and Lowry's definitions of acids and bases differ from the Arrhenius definition?

ANSWERS ➤ 391

CHECK YOUR ANSWERS

1. Acids are substances that dissociate in water to produce hydrogen ions.

2. Bases are substances that dissociate in water to produce hydroxide ions.

3. Neutralization occurs when an acid and base mix and the hydrogen ions and hydroxide ions combine to produce water.

4. For an acid, blue litmus will turn red, and red litmus will stay red. For a base, blue litmus stays blue, and red litmus turns blue.

5. Both acids and bases conduct electricity in an aqueous solution.

6. A salt is the result of an acid and a base reacting.

7. Bronsted and Lowry defined acids and bases by their ability to accept or donate a proton, while the Arrhenius definition explained acids and bases that contained hydrogen and hydroxide ions.

Chapter 29

pH SCALE AND CALCULATIONS

The concentration of hydrogen ions and hydroxide ions in an aqueous solution containing an acid or base indicates the strength of the solution. The concentrations are usually so small that it's difficult to read them.

THE pH SCALE

In 1909, SOREN SORENSON, a Danish biochemist, came up with a way of simplifying and identifying the concentration of acidity or base in a solution: pH. **pH** is an advanced algebra function called the "p-function," which means "take the negative of the base 10 logarithm." The pH scale was created so that people could easily see the degree of acidity or **ALKALINITY** (base) in a substance.

The pH scale ranges from 0 to 14. Any substance that is a 7 is considered to be neutral, meaning that it is neither an acid nor a base.

Common Substances and Their pH Values

	pH	EXAMPLE
increasingly acidic	0	battery acid
	1	gastric acid
	2	lemon juice, vinegar
Acids have a pH < 7.	3	soda
	4	tomato juice
	5	bananas
	6	milk
A pH of 7 is neutral. neutral	7	water
	8	eggs
	9	baking soda
Bases have a pH > 7.	10	milk of magnesia
	11	ammonia solution
	12	soapy water
	13	bleach
increasingly alkaline	14	drain cleaner

pH is a measure of the acidity or amount of hydrogen ions (H^+) in a solution (in moles per liter).

The equation used to show this is

$$pH = -\log[H^+]$$

Square brackets represent molarity.

This is read as "**pH is equal to the negative log of a certain number of hydrogen ions.**" pH is base 10 log.

What is a log?

"Log" is short for LOGARITHM. A logarithm is a mathematical action that tells how many times the base is multiplied by itself to reach that number. It answers the question: *How many times do I have to multiply one number (a base) to get another number?*

FOR EXAMPLE: How many 2s do I multiply to get 8? $2 \times 2 \times 2$, or $2^3 = 8$. This would be written as $\log_2(8) = 3$. We read this as "**log base 2 of 8 is 3.**"

Base

Nope.

$\log_2(8) = 3$

This one.

Chemists use logarithms for pH because sometimes the number of hydrogens in one substance can be one trillion (1,000,000,000,000, or one million million) times different from another substance.

1,000,000,000,000 expressed as an exponent is 10^{12}, which is much easier to write.

CALCULATING pH AND pOH OF STRONG ACIDS AND BASES

Chemists sometimes need to calculate the pH of a solution based on an experiment that they are performing. They need to know the molarity of the solution. The pH tells you the negative log of the concentration of the H^+ ions, and you have to solve for concentration from the formula. If you have a base, you will need to determine the negative (-) log of the concentration of OH^- ions. For that, you need to find the pOH, which is the pH of the -log of the concentration of the hydroxide ions.

$$pOH = -\log[OH^-]$$

If you know the pOH, use this equation to solve for the [OH⁻]:

$$[OH^-] = 10^{-pOH}$$

pH = -log[H⁺]

If you know the pH, then you use this equation to solve for the [H⁺]:

$$[H^+] = 10^{-pH}$$

At 25°C, the relationship between pH and pOH is:

pH + pOH = 14.00

pH and pOH change when temperature changes, so 25°C is usually used as the standard temperature for most problems.

If you start with pH = $-\log[H^+]$, divide each side by -1 so that you have $-pH = \log[H^+]$. Then, apply base 10 to each side, the "10 to the log" cancels out, and the result is $10^{-pH} = [H^+]$.

The concentration of a nitric acid solution is 2.1×10^{-4} M. What is the pH of the solution?

$pH = -\log [H^+]$
$pH = -\log [2.1 \times 10^{-4}] = 3.68$

The pH of the solution is 3.7. This is an acidic solution.

> Nitric acid (HNO_3) is a strong acid, meaning that it dissociates by 100%. So, the concentration of H^+ ions (required by the equation) is considered to be equal to the initial concentration of the HNO_3 itself. The molarity of the HNO_3 solution is the molarity of the H^+ ions.

If the pOH of an ammonium hydroxide solution is 8.6, calculate the molarity of OH^- ions in the solution.

$pOH = -\log [OH^-]$

$[OH^-] = 10^{-pOH} = 10^{-8.6} = 2.5 \times 10^{-9}$ M

pOH is equal to 8.6 so it becomes the superscript to the 10th exponent.

The concentration of a sodium hydroxide (NaOH) solution is 4.56×10^{-4} M. Calculate the pH of the solution.

NaOH is a base. So the molarity calculated is equal to [OH⁻].

1. Find the pOH.

$$pOH = -\log [OH^-] = -\log [4.56 \times 10^{-4}] = 3.341$$

2. Find the pH.

$$pH = 14.00 - pOH = 14.00 - 3.34 = 10.66$$

CHECK: Is the pH greater than 7? It should be, because NaOH is a base.

Normal rain is slightly acidic and has a pH of 5.6. This is because the carbon dioxide reacts with water in the air to form a weak carbonic acid, shown as:

$$CO_2 + H_2O \rightleftharpoons H_2CO_3$$

Sulfur dioxide mixes with oxygen in the atmosphere to create a sulfate ion,

$$2\,SO_2 + O_2 \rightleftharpoons 2\,SO_3^-,$$

that when mixed with water leads to

$$SO_3^- + H_2O \rightleftharpoons H_2SO_4 \text{ (sulfuric acid)}.$$

But when sulfuric acid is added into the rain, it causes this reaction:

$$H_2SO_4 \rightarrow 2H^+ + SO_4^{2-},$$

which creates acid rain. With a pH of 4.2 to 4.4, acid rain can cause damage to plants and animals, and even statues and buildings.

FOR EXAMPLE: Calculate the pH of a strong base solution.

If you use 0.5 g of potassium hydroxide (KOH) to make a total of 2.5 L of aqueous solution, what will be the pH?

1. Write the dissociation equation to determine the relationship between the reactant and the $[OH^-]$.

$$pOH = -\log [OH^-]$$

$$KOH \rightarrow K^+ + OH^-$$

In this case, 1 mol KOH produces 1 mol OH^-.

2. Determine the concentration of hydroxide ions $[OH^-]$.

$$0.50 \text{ g KOH} \times \frac{1 \text{ mol KOH}}{56.11 \text{ g/mol}} = \frac{0.0089}{2.5 \text{ L}} = 0.0036 \text{ M}$$

.50 g of KOH is given in the problem.

Convert g KOH to mol KOH.

Divide mol KOH by the given volume to get molarity.

> The significant figures in pH start after the decimal.
> The whole number before the decimal only corresponds
> to the exponent of the concentration, so it doesn't count.

3. Find the pOH.

$$pOH = -\log(.0036) = 2.44$$

4. Solve for pH.

$$pH = 14 - 2.44 = 11.56$$

pH in our lives

Some plants, like radishes, sweet potatoes, and blueberries, love acidic soil. They prefer soil with a pH between 4.0 and 5.5.

Each type of food is required to meet a certain pH for it to be sold. The pH is determined by the flavor that is desired. Even a slight change to the pH can cause the food to taste bitter or sour.

Shampoo is required to have a specific pH to be sold.

CHECK YOUR KNOWLEDGE

1. What is pH?

2. What does the pH range tell you?

3. What is pOH and how is it related to pH?

4. Calculate the pOH and pH of a .076 M NaOH solution.

5. Was your answer to #4 correct? How would you check to make sure that it was?

6. Calculate the H⁺ concentration in a solution that has a pH of 5.0.

7. Calculate the grams of KOH needed to prepare 768 mL of solution with a pH of 11.0.

ANSWERS   403

CHECK YOUR ANSWERS

1. pH is a measure of hydrogen ions (H^+) in a solution (in mol/liter). It is a negative logarithmic relationship. (It does not directly equate to H^+ ions.)

2. Acids have a pH < 7, bases have a pH > 7, and a pH of 7 is neutral.

3. pOH is the negative log of the concentration of OH^- ions. At 25°C, the relationship between pH and pOH is pH + pOH = 14.00.

4. $pOH = -\log [OH^-] = -\log [.076] = 1.12$

   $pH = 14.00 - 1.12 = 12.88$

5. To check your answer, you would see if the pH is greater than 7. That means that the sodium hydroxide solution is a base, which is true.

6. $[H^+] = 10^{-pH} = 10^{-5.0} = .000010$ M (check the zeroes)

7. $pOH = 3.0 \ [OH^-] = 10^{-pOH} = 10^{-3.0}$

   10^{-3} M $\times$ 0.768 L = 7.68×10^{-4} mol $\times$ 56.1 g/mol = 0.043 g

Chapter 30

CONJUGATE ACIDS AND BASES

When acids and bases react, they reach **CHEMICAL EQUILIBRIUM** —a point where the reaction is reversible, and the products and reactants are reacting at the same speed to establish a ratio of concentration of products/ reactants. The ratio reaches a constant value. Many chemical reactions are reversible.

> the products can re-form into the reactants

A **FORWARD REACTION** is indicated by an arrow pointing from left to right: $\longrightarrow$

A **REVERSE REACTION** has an arrow that points from right to left: $\longleftarrow$

When you put them together, that creates a double arrow, ⇌, which indicates chemical equilibrium.

In this reaction, A is an acid:

$$HA + H_2O \rightleftharpoons H_3O^+ + A^-$$

The acid (A) gives away a proton, and the base accepts a proton. In the forward reaction of this experiment, hyaluronic acid (HA) donates a proton to H_2O, turning it into H_3O^+. That means that water is the base, because it accepts a proton.

In the reverse reaction, the A^- becomes the base and the hydronium ion (H_3O^+) is the acid. Hydronium donates a proton to the A to form HA.

The two parts of the reaction that lose and gain a proton are **CONJUGATE PAIRS**.

CONJUGATE PAIRS
One acid and one base that differ from each other by the presence or absence of one hydrogen ion that has transferred between them.

one conjugate pair

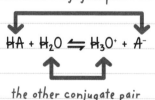

$$HA + H_2O \rightleftharpoons H_3O^+ + A^-$$

the other conjugate pair

Conjugate pairs differ in their formulas by exactly one proton.

HA and A are conjugate pairs because they are changed by the acceptance or donation of one proton.

H_2O and H_3O^+ are conjugate pairs because they are changed by the acceptance or donation of one proton.

EQUILIBRIUM REACTION
Occurs when the rate of the forward reaction is equal to the rate of the reverse reaction.

FOR EXAMPLE: Given the following reaction, determine its conjugate pairs:

$$NH_3 + H_2O \rightleftharpoons NH_4^+ + OH^-$$

1. Identify the compounds that donate a proton and those that accept a proton.

   NH_3 becomes NH_4^+ so it accepts a proton. That makes it a **base**.

   H_2O becomes OH^-, so it donates a proton. This makes it an **acid**.

   NH_4^+ donates a proton in the reverse reaction, and this makes it an **acid**.

OH⁻ accepts a proton in the reverse reaction, and this makes it a **base**.

2. Ask: Is the reaction reversible? Yes, because the double arrow ⇌ makes the conjugate pairs:

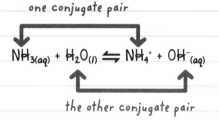

one conjugate pair

$$NH_{3(aq)} + H_2O_{(l)} \rightleftharpoons NH_4^+ + OH^-_{(aq)}$$

the other conjugate pair

The reaction will form the weaker base, NH_4OH, and the weaker acid, NH_3.

FOR EXAMPLE: Identify the conjugate pairs in the following reactions:

$$H_2PO_4^- + NH_3 \rightleftharpoons HPO_4^{2-} + NH_4^+$$

NH_3 acts as a base because it accepts a proton from $H_2PO_4^-$. HPO_4^{2-} is basic and accepts a proton from NH_4^+, which is acting as an acid. This makes NH_3/NH_4^+ an acid-base pair because they differ by one proton. $H_2PO_4^-$ and HPO_4^{2-} are also an acid-base pair.

$$HClO + CH_3NH_2 \rightleftharpoons CH_3NH_3^+ + ClO^-$$

HClO is acting as the acid and donating the proton to form ClO^-, a base; CH_3NH_2 is a base accepting a proton to become $CH_3NH_3^+$, an acid.

Water can act as a base in one reaction and as an acid in another. Substances that can act as both acids and bases are **AMPHOTERIC**. Other examples of amphoteric substances include polyatomic ions that contain both an H^+ and a negative charge in their formulas. They can both donate the H^+ and accept an H^+.

STRENGTH OF ACIDS AND BASES

Chemists use an **ACID DISSOCIATION CONSTANT** (or K_a), to determine the strength of an acid. The more ions that an acid has, the stronger an electrolyte it will be, and the higher the ratio of ions to reactants.

K_a is also known as the ACID IONIZATION CONSTANT or the ACIDITY CONSTANT.

The formula to find K_a:

$$K_a = \frac{[\text{products}]}{[\text{reactants}]}$$

For example: $HA + H_2O \rightleftharpoons H_3O^+ + A^-$

Note: Solids and pure liquids, like water, are not included in K_a expressions because their concentrations are constant.

$$K_a = \frac{[H_3O^+]\,[A^-]}{[HA]}$$

The brackets indicate the molarity of each of the substances. Sometimes, the concentrations are extremely small, like 10^{-3} or 10^{-6}. That makes K_a tiny.

The strength and molarity of the acid determine the acid's K_a. An acid can be strong but diluted, or weak but concentrated.

A strong acid almost completely dissociates in water and has a large K_a (a value greater than 1). A weak acid does not completely dissociate in water and has a small K_a (a value of less than 1).

Types of acids and their conjugate bases:

ACID	CONJUGATE BASE
Strong Acids	
HCl (hydrochloric acid) (strongest)	Cl^- (chloride ion) (weakest)
H_2SO_4 (sulfuric acid)	HSO_4^-; SO_4^{2-} forms two conjugate bases as hydrogen ions are successively removed from the acids
HNO_3 (nitric acid)	NO^{3-} (nitrate ion)
Weak Acids	
H_3PO_4 (phosphoric acid)	$H_2PO_4^-$ (dihydrogen phosphate ion)
CH_3COOH (acetic acid)	CH_3COO^- (acetate ion)
H_2CO_3 (carbonic acid)	HCO_3^- (hydrogen carbonate ion)
HCN (hydrocyanic acid) (weakest)	CN^- (cyanide ion) (strongest)

CHECK YOUR KNOWLEDGE

1. What is the difference between an Arrhenius acid and an Arrhenius base?

2. What is a conjugate pair and in what type of reaction is it found?

3. What is the conjugate acid or the conjugate base of the following?

    A. HF
    B. CH_3COOH
    C. NO_3^-
    D. HCO_3^-

4. What is the acid dissociation constant?

5. What does the term *amphoteric* describe? What substance can be categorized as amphoteric?

6. In the reaction $H_2PO_4^- + NH_3 \rightleftharpoons HPO_4^{2-} + NH_4^+$, $H_2PO_4^-$ and HPO_4^{2-} are considered an acid-base pair because _____.

CHECK YOUR ANSWERS

1. Arrhenius acids are substances that dissociate in water to produce hydrogen (H^+) ions. Arrhenius bases break up in water to produce hydroxide (OH^-) ions.

2. Conjugate pairs are the combination of one acid and one base that differ from each other by the presence or absence of the hydrogen ion that has transferred between them. They are only found in reversible equilibrium reactions.

3. **A.** F^- is the conjugate base after the HF acid loses an H^+.
   B. CH_3COO^- is the conjugate base after the CH_3COOH loses an H+.
   C. HNO_3 is the conjugate acid after NO_3^- accepts an H^+.
   D. H_2CO_3 is the conjugate acid after HCO_3^- accepts an H^+.

4. The acid dissociation constant is the measure of the strength of an acid in a solution.

5. The term *amphoteric* describes substances that can act as both acids and bases.

6. $H_2PO_4^-$ and HPO_4^{2-} are considered an acid–base pair because they differ by one proton.

Chapter 31

TITRATIONS

FINDING CONCENTRATIONS

A **TITRATION** determines the concentration of an unknown solution. During a titration, the **TITRANT**, or reagent (a solution with a known concentration), is slowly added (or titrated) into a solution of unknown concentration until the endpoint of the reaction is reached. The endpoint is reached when a color change has occurred. If you know the concentration of one of the solutions, you can calculate the concentration of the other.

Titration setup:

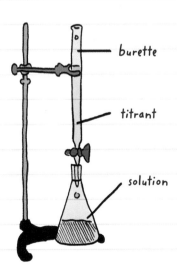

burette

titrant

solution

The burette contains the solution of known (standardized) concentration. The concentration of the solution in the flask is unknown. An **INDICATOR** is added to the solution in the flask and lets the chemist know when to stop the titration, because it causes a color change when moles are equal. The resulting solution is known as the **STANDARDIZED SOLUTION**, because its molarity is determined mathematically after the titration.

During a titration, the reagent is added slowly so that you can see the first moment that the indicator changes color. Sometimes, that means adding one drop of the reagent at a time when approaching the endpoint.

INDICATOR
A substance that changes color to indicate a change in pH. For acid-base titrations, it is usually phenolphthalein (ppth), which changes from colorless to pink at a pH of about 8.1.

TITRATION CALCULATIONS

FOR EXAMPLE: A 45.00 mL solution of 0.20 M sodium hydroxide (NaOH) is needed to neutralize 25.00 mL of hydrochloric acid (HCl solution). What is the concentration (in molarity) of the HCl solution?

1. Write a balanced chemical equation for the neutralization reaction.

An acid and a base will combine to form a salt. The salt formed must be sodium chloride, NaCl.

Look for the point at which the moles of H^+ = the moles of OH^-.

Write a net ionic equation:

NAOH + HCL → NACL + H₂O

2. Calculate the number of moles of HCl that are consumed in the reaction.

$$0.0450 \text{ L NaOH} \times \frac{0.20 \text{ mol}}{1 \text{ L NaOH}} \times \frac{1 \text{ mol HCl}}{1 \text{ mol NaOH}} = .0090 \text{ mol HCl}$$

3. Convert to molarity of HCl.

The stoichiometry of the balanced equation tells us that 1 mol NaOH reacts with 1 mol HCl.

4. Calculate the molarity of HCl.

$$\frac{.0090 \text{ mol HCl}}{.02500 \text{ L HCl}} = 0.36 \text{ M HCl}$$

Titration stoichiometry can be summarized as

$$M_a V_a = M_b V_b$$

only if the acid and base react in a one-to-one ratio.

M_a = molarity of acid   (HCL = x)
V_a = volume of acid   (HCL = 25 mL)
M_b = molarity of base   (NaOH = 0.20)
V_b = volume of base   (NaOH = 45 mL)

The previous example could have also been set up as:

$(x)(25) = (.2)(45)$
$25x = 9.0$
$x = .36$ M   **Note:** For this calculation, the volume can
                     be in milliliters as long as both volumes are
                     in milliliters.

CHECK YOUR KNOWLEDGE

1. What is the purpose of performing a titration?

2. Describe the setup of a titration experiment.

3. What is an indicator and why is it important?

4. Why is accuracy so important during a titration?

5. Which of the two solutions is known as the standardizing solution?

6. How would you prepare 500 mL of a .40 M sulfuric acid solution from a stock solution of 2.5 M sulfuric acid?

7. A 50.0 mL sample of HCl is titrated to the endpoint with 25.00 mL of a .50 M NaOH solution. What is the concentration of the HCl?

ANSWERS ⟶

CHECK YOUR ANSWERS

1. A titration is an experiment performed to determine the concentration of an unknown solution.

2. A solution of known concentration is placed into a burette and slowly added to a solution of unknown concentration in the beaker or flask below it.

3. An indicator is a substance that changes color to indicate when the reaction has reached the endpoint; that is, the moles of reacting substances are equal. For an acid-base titration, this point is usually signified by a change in color and in pH.

4. The very first color change signifies the end of the reaction. If you overshoot the endpoint, you may have to repeat the titration experiment again, because you will have passed the point at which moles of reacting substances are equal.

5. The solution of known concentration is contained in the burette. In this solution, you already know the amount and concentration with accuracy.

6. $M_1 V_1 = M_2 V_2$

$(2.5)(x) = (.4)(500) = 80$ mL. Measure 80.0 mL of 2.5 M sulfuric acid in a pipette. Place a small amount of water in a volumetric flask and then add the concentrated acid. (Always be careful when adding acid to water.) Last, add water until the bottom of the meniscus (the curved upper surface of the liquid) rests on the measurement line of a 500 mL volumetric flask.

7. $M_a V_a = M_b V_b$

$(x)(50) = (.5)(25) = .25$ M HCl

Unit 11

Chemical Compounds

Chapter 32

CHEMICAL EQUILIBRIUM

CHEMICAL EQUILIBRIUM

Many chemical reactions are reversible. That means that they proceed in both directions: The conversion of reactants to products and of products to reactants happens at the same time.

Chemical equilibrium is a dynamic process, meaning that it keeps changing. A reaction can proceed in the forward direction, the reverse, or both. A reaction can also be "shifted" to favor one direction over the other by manipulating conditions.

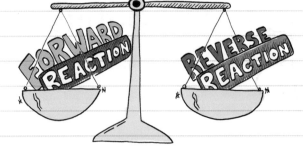

Reversible reaction:

$A + B \rightarrow C + D$ (forward reaction)

$A + B \leftarrow C + D$ (reverse reaction)

An **equilibrium reaction:**

$A + B \rightleftharpoons C + D$

> Chemical equilibrium is achieved when the rates of the
> forward reaction and reverse reaction are equal, and the
> ratio of products to reactants remains constant.

Examples of equilibrium reactions:

PRECIPITATION REACTION

$$Ca^{2+} + 2OH^- \rightarrow Ca(OH)_{2(s)}$$

The calcium ion is added to two hydroxide ions to form
calcium hydroxide as a precipitate.

ACID-BASE REACTIONS

Weak acids and bases undergo equilibrium. Strong acids and bases dissociate 100% and are considered to be "one-way" reactions.

For example:

$$NaOH_{(aq)} + HCl_{(aq)} \rightarrow NaCl_{(s)} + H_2O$$

Sodium hydroxide combines with hydrochloric acid to produce sodium chloride and water. Hydrochloric acid is a strong acid (and NaOH is a strong base) and dissociates completely, so the equation goes in only one direction.

$$NH_3 + H_2O \rightleftharpoons NH_4^+ + OH^-$$

Ammonia is a weak acid and does not dissociate completely into water to form ammonium ions and hydroxide ions. This means that the reaction is reversible.

REDOX REACTIONS

These are oxidizing-reduction reactions, where the oxidation number of a molecule, atom, or ion changes by either gaining or losing an electron.

For example: $2Fe^{3+}_{(aq)} + Zn_{(s)} \rightleftharpoons 2Fe^{2+}_{(aq)} + Zn^{2+}_{(aq)}$

Two ions of Fe (III) combine with zinc in an aqueous solution to form two ions of Fe (II) and one ion of zinc. The zinc donated two electrons, one to each of the Fe (III) ions, and this turns them into two Fe (II) ions.

CHEMICAL AND PHYSICAL EQUILIBRIUM

A **CHEMICAL EQUILIBRIUM REACTION** has different substances for the reactants and products.

For example: $HNO_2 \rightleftharpoons H^+ + NO_2^-$

PHYSICAL EQUILIBRIUM REACTIONS have one substance that changes phase (it moves, in some combination, from solid to liquid to gas).

In this equation, water moves from liquid to gas in a physical equilibrium reaction:

$$H_2O_{(l)} \rightleftharpoons H_2O_{(g)}$$

Chemists use chemical equilibrium reactions to predict how reactants will behave in a **CLOSED SYSTEM**. The system is the environment being studied.

Conditions for equilibrium:

- Equilibrium can only be obtained in a closed system.

- The rate of the forward reaction is equal to the rate of the reverse reaction.

> **CLOSED SYSTEM**
> No substances are added or removed from the system, but energy can be transferred in or out.

- **CATALYSTS** do not shift the position of equilibrium, but they increase the rate at which equilibrium is achieved.

- The concentration of the reactants and products remain constant but are not necessarily equal.

> **CATALYST**
> A substance that can affect the rate of a chemical reaction without being changed itself.

There are three systems:

An **open system** allows for free exchange of matter and energy.

A **closed system** only allows for exchange of energy.

An **isolated system** does not allow any exchange.

In this reaction, a color change occurs, showing that a reaction is taking place:

$$N_2O_{4(g)} \rightleftharpoons 2NO_{2(g)}$$

(colorless gas)   (brown gas)

Dinitrogen tetraoxide (N_2O_4) is a colorless gas. Nitrogen dioxide (NO_2) is a brown gas. When dinitrogen tetraoxide is injected into an empty flask, some of it immediately starts to turn brown. This indicates that it is forming nitrogen dioxide. As the reaction continues, the brown color gets increasingly darker and then begins to fade slightly.

The fading happens because some of the nitrogen dioxide is turning back into dinitrogen tetraoxide (the reverse reaction). The reaction continues until a constant light-brown color is reached, signaling equilibrium.

THE EQUILIBRIUM CONSTANT

Chemists want to be able to determine the concentration of each of the products and reactants at any time during an equilibrium reaction.

The ratio of the concentrations of products to reactants in an equilibrium system is called the **EQUILIBRIUM CONSTANT, K**.

The equilibrium constant is the mathematical expression of the LAW OF MASS ACTION, which states that for a reversible reaction at a constant temperature, the ratio of reactant to product concentrations has a constant value, K.

$$K = \frac{[\text{products}]}{[\text{reactants}]}$$

The square brackets represent molarity (mole/liter), which can apply to solutions and gases.

In these reactions, $aA + bB \rightleftharpoons cC + dD$.

$$K = \frac{[C]^c [D]^d}{[A]^a [B]^b}$$

if $K > 1$, the equilibrium is on the side of the products;

if $K < 1$, there is a higher concentration of reactants than products;

if $K = 1$, concentrations of the products and reactants are equal.

The coefficients of the balanced equation become exponents in the K expression.

There are different equilibrium constants for different reactions.

a = acid
b = base
c = concentration
p = pressure
K_{sp} = the solubility product
K_w = ion constant for water

- K_a = acid dissociation constant

$$= \frac{[H_3O^+] [A^-]}{[HA]}$$

for this reaction:

$HA + H_2O \rightleftharpoons H_3O^+ + A^-$

- K_b = base dissociation constant = $\dfrac{[B^-][OH^-]}{[BOH]}$

for this reaction: $BOH \rightleftharpoons B^+ + OH^-$

- K_a and K_b are related to each other by the ion constant for water K_w, where $K_w = 1.0 \times 10^{-14}$

$$K_w = K_a \times K_b$$

- K_c and K_p are equilibrium constants of gas mixtures, although K_c can also be used for reactions occurring in aqueous solutions, such as complex ion reactions.

For the equation $aA_{(g)} + bB_{(g)} \rightleftharpoons cC_{(g)} + dD_{(g)}$,

K_c uses molar concentrations (shown by the brackets [ ]) and can be used for solution equilibria or gas equilibria:

$$K_c = \dfrac{[C]^c \, [D]^d}{[A]^a \, [B]^b}$$

K_p uses partial pressures of the gases in a closed system, shown by P and parentheses: $P(\ )$.

$$K_p = \dfrac{P(C)^c \, P(D)^d}{P(A)^a \, P(B)^b}$$

The relationship between K_c and K_p depends on the type of system.

In **homogeneous equilibrium**, all reacting species are in the same phase (i.e., gas). **This equation is only for gas equilbrium reactions.**

FOR EXAMPLE: Write the expressions for k_c and/or k_p.

- $HF_{(aq)} + H_2O_{(l)} \rightleftharpoons H_3O^+_{(aq)} + F^-_{(aq)}$

You only determine k_c, because this is not a gaseous mixture.

$$k_c = \frac{[H_3O^+][F^-]}{[HF]}$$

No solids or liquids (including water) in *K* expressions.

- $2CO_{2(g)} \rightleftharpoons 2CO_{(g)} + O_{2(g)}$

$$k_c = \frac{[CO]^2[O_2]}{[CO_2]^2} \text{ and } k_p = \frac{(PCO)^2(PO_2)}{(PCO_2)^2}$$

FOR EXAMPLE: In the following reaction,
$2NO_{(g)} + O_{2(g)} \rightleftharpoons 2NO_{2(g)},$

solve for k_p given that the temperature is 315k.
$$k_p = k_c(RT)^{\Delta n}.$$

$n = 2$ moles of product gas – 3 moles of reactant gas = –1

$$k_p = (.0821)^{-1}(5.35 \times 10^4)(315°k) = 3.14 \times 10^6$$

Because solids are not included in K expressions, a solubility product, or K_{sp}, for solutions must be found.

K vs Q

Because equilibrium reactions are reversible, sometimes chemists want to know which side of the reaction is favored.

K_{sp} is the solubility product for dissociation reactions. It is equal to the product of solubilities of the products of a dissociation reaction.

For the reaction $Mg(OH)_{2(s)} \rightleftharpoons Mg^{2+} + 2OH^-$

$$K_{sp} = [Mg^{+2}][OH^-]^2$$

Chemists need to know, given initial amounts of substances involved, does the reaction proceed toward products or will it favor the reactants? K is the equilibrium constant, and it helps to answer that question.

K predicts a point of equilibrium, where the rate of the forward and reverse reactions are equal. The **REACTION QUOTIENT (Q)** tells you, based on any given INITIAL combination of concentrations of reactants and products, how the reaction will proceed toward equilibrium.

For this equation, $aA_{(g)} + bB_{(g)} \rightleftharpoons cC_{(g)} + dD_{(g)}$,

$$Q = \frac{[C]^c\,[D]^d}{[A]^a\,[B]^b}$$

The equation to find Q is the same equation as K, BUT in the equation solving for Q, concentrations are all initial concentrations, **not** equilibrium concentrations.

Q is like a snapshot in time of K.

If $Q > K$, the reaction proceeds toward the reactants. The system shifts LEFT ← to make more reactants.

If $Q < K$, the reaction proceeds toward the products. The system shifts RIGHT → to make more products.

If $Q = K$, the reaction is already at equilibrium.

FOR EXAMPLE: At the start of this reaction, $2SO_{2(g)} + O_{2(g)} \rightleftharpoons 2SO_3$, the initial amounts of gases (in moles) are .35 mol SO_2, 3.25×10^{-2} mol O_2, and 6.41×10^{-4} mol SO_3 in a 4.50 L solution.

If the K_c for this reaction is 3.5 at room temperature, determine whether this system is at equilibrium. If it is not, predict which way the reaction will proceed.

1. Find the initial concentration molarity of each substance.

$$\frac{.35 \text{ mol } SO_2}{4.50 \text{ L}} = .078 \text{ M } SO_2$$

$$\frac{3.25 \times 10^{-2} \text{ mol } O_2}{4.50 \text{ L}} = .00722 \text{ M } O_2$$

$$\frac{6.41 \times 10^{-4} \text{ mol } SO_3}{4.50 \text{ L}} = .000142 \text{ M } SO_3$$

2. Solve for Q.

$$Q = \frac{[SO_3]^2}{[SO_2]^2[O_2]} = \frac{[0.000142]^2}{[.078]^2[.00722]} = 4.6 \times 10^{-4}$$

$Q < K$ therefore there are too many reactants and not enough products, so the reaction will shift right.

436

CONCENTRATION vs TIME GRAPHS

You can see how a reaction will progress by looking at its concentration vs time graph.

This graph shows the equilibrium occurring in the reversible reaction by the joined (purple) straight line. That's because at equilibrium, the reaction rate of both the forward and reverse reactions is the same.

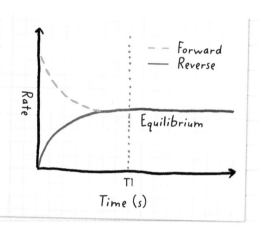

This graph shows concentration vs time plotted. The amount of reactants starts high and then tapers off. That's because the reactants are being used up. The initial amount of

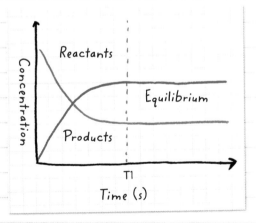

products is low and increases as products are created. The straight lines of the reactants and products show that the reaction has reached equilibrium.

In this graph, more reactants are produced than products at equilibrium.

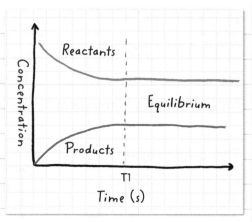

A real-life example of chemical equilibrium can be found in the human body. Hemoglobin (Hb) in the blood binds to oxygen (O_2) in red blood cells from the lungs and is transported through the body via red blood cells. When the mixture reaches a part of the body that needs oxygen, oxygen leaves the red blood cell and goes into the tissue. As long as oxygen is available in the lungs, this equilibrium continues. But if a person were to go high up in the mountains where atmospheric pressure is lower, less oxygen is available to bond with the hemoglobin and the reaction shifts left, toward the separated hemoglobin and oxygen and away from the product, oxygenated hemoglobin. The physical result of the shift is that the person may feel light-headed.

CHECK YOUR KNOWLEDGE

1. What type of process is an equilibrium reaction? Give an example of two types reactions that may be at equilibrium.

2. What is the difference between a chemical equilibrium reaction and a physical equilibrium reaction?

3. What are the three different kinds of systems that you can have? Explain how they each deal with energy and the surrounding environment.

4. Define K_w, K_a, and K_b. Tell how they are mathematically related.

5. What are K_c and K_p?

6. What is Q? If $Q > K$, what does that tell you about the reaction?

ANSWERS   439

1. Chemical equilibrium is a dynamic process, meaning that the reactions within a system can go in the forward direction, the reverse, or both. Examples of equilibrium reactions are precipitation, weak acid-base, redox, and gas.

2. A chemical equilibrium reaction has different substances for the reactants and products. But physical equilibrium reactions have one substance that changes phase (it moves in some combination from solid to liquid to gas).

3. An open system allows for free exchange of matter and energy. A closed system only allows for exchange of energy. An isolated system does not allow any exchange.

4. K_w = the equilibrium constant for water, K_a = equilibrium constant for acids, K_b = equilibrium constant for bases. $K_w = K_a \times K_b$

5. K_c and K_p are constants of gas mixtures. K_c uses molar concentrations, denoted by brackets [ ]. K_p uses partial pressures of the gases in a closed system, denoted by parentheses ( ).

6. Q is the reaction quotient, similar to K but at initial conditions. If $Q > K$, the reaction favors the reactants. The system shifts LEFT (←) to make more reactants.

Chapter 33

LE CHÂTELIER'S PRINCIPLE

Reversible reactions in equilibrium can shift due to factors that include:

- temperature
- volume
- pressure
- concentration

LE CHÂTELIER'S PRINCIPLE can be used to predict the effect that a change in one of these factors will have on the system.

HENRY LOUIS LE CHÂTELIER was a French chemist who devised a way to predict the effect that a changing condition has on a system in chemical equilibrium. He called it LE CHÂTELIER'S PRINCIPLE.

> **Le Châtelier's Principle** states that if an external stress is applied to a system at equilibrium, the system will adjust to reestablish a new equilibrium. The system will shift in the direction that relieves the stress, to reduce the stressor.

The principle explains that equilibrium reactions are self-correcting. If reactions are thrown out of equilibrium, or balance, they will shift in one direction to get back into equilibrium.

CHANGING CONCENTRATION

Given the reaction

$$2A_{(aq)} + B_{(aq)} \rightleftharpoons C_{(aq)} + 2D_{(aq)},$$

- What happens if you increase the concentration of A?

The reaction will *shift RIGHT* to form more products because a stress has been placed on the reactant side, causing the extra particles of A to collide with B and make C and D.

- What happens if you decrease the concentration of B?

The reaction will *shift LEFT* to form more reactants because the reactant has been removed; the system will compensate to replace it by converting product into reactant.

🔹 What happens if you remove C from the reaction as soon as it is formed?

The reaction will *shift RIGHT* to form more products, **which will mean more C.**

🔹 What will happen if you add a common ion of another compound to the original solution?

$$FeSCN^-_{(aq)} \rightleftharpoons Fe^{3+}_{(aq)} + SCN^-_{(aq)}$$

What will happen if you add NaSCN to this solution?

The NaSCN will dissociate to form more SCN⁻ ions, which creates an excess of SCN⁻ in the system. This will cause the reaction to *shift LEFT* to create more reactants.

If you **T**ake a substance, the reactions shifts **T**oward that substance to restore it.

If you **A**dd a substance, the reaction will shift **A**way from that substance to remove it.

Changing Pressure

Changes in pressure only affect reactions that are gaseous.

Using this reaction, assume these are all gases:

$$2A_{(g)} + B_{(g)} \rightleftharpoons C_{(g)} + D_{(g)}$$

● What will happen if the pressure is increased?

There are three molecules of gas on the left-hand side and two molecules of gas on the right of the reaction. The reaction will shift in a direction that is least affected by the stress, so that the pressure is reduced. That means that the reaction will *shift RIGHT* toward the product side, where there are fewer gas molecules (the fewer the gas molecules, the lower the pressure).

● What will happen if the pressure is decreased?

The reaction will *shift LEFT* to form more gas molecules (the more gas molecules, the higher the pressure).

● What will happen if the moles of gas are equal on both sides?

There will be *no shift.* The entire system will just be under more pressure.

The beakers below illustrate the reaction $3H_{2(g)} + N_{2(g)} \rightleftharpoons 2NH_{3(g)}$

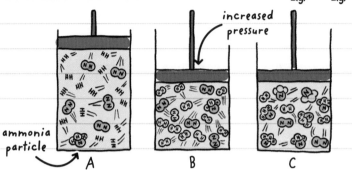

In beaker A there are five molecules of nitrogen and fourteen molecules of hydrogen, for a total of nineteen gas particles of reactants. There is only one ammonia particle, which represents the products.

As the pressure is increased in beaker B, the particles move closer together and collide to react more often.

Beaker C shows that the new equilibrium has more ammonia particles because that reduces the total particles in the system.

Changing Volume

Changing the volume of a gaseous equilibrium system has the same effect as changing the pressure. The change is determined by the number of moles of each substance present.

- What happens if there are the same number of moles/ molecules on each side of the equilibrium reaction? In this case, changing the pressure or volume has NO effect.

Changing Temperature

If energy is used (absorbed) by the reactant to create the product, then the reaction is **ENDOTHERMIC**.

> In an **endothermic** reaction, **heat is a reactant**.
> In an **exothermic** reaction, **heat is a product**.

If energy was given off (released) during the creation of the product, then the reaction is **EXOTHERMIC**.

Energy is measured in kJ (KILOJOULES) and is shown by $\blacktriangle H$ for ENTHALPY.

> $\blacktriangle H$, or **enthalpy**, reflects the amount of heat given off or absorbed in a reaction carried out at constant pressure.

released

250 kJ is **evolved** when A and B react completely to give C and D.

$A + 2B \rightleftharpoons C + D \quad \blacktriangle H = -250 \ kJ \ mol^{-1}$

250 kJ is **absorbed** when C and D react completely to give A and B.

■ What happens if you increase the temperature in a reaction?

If you use the above equation and increase the heat, the reaction would *shift LEFT* to absorb more heat.

● What happens if you decrease the temperature in a reaction?

In the reaction above, if you decrease the heat, the reaction would shift RIGHT to release more heat.

Things to know!

⬆ The temperature of a system in dynamic equilibrium **favors the endothermic reaction and will increase the yield of the forward reaction.** The system counteracts the change that you have made by absorbing the extra heat. (Favors means that you will make more product.)

⬇ The temperature of a system in dynamic equilibrium **favors the exothermic reaction.** The system counteracts the change that you have made by producing more heat and shifting to the right to create more product.

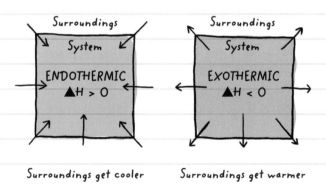

Surroundings get cooler   Surroundings get warmer

CHECK YOUR KNOWLEDGE

1. What is Le Châtelier's Principle?

2. If you have the reaction $2A_{(g)} + B_{(g)} \rightleftharpoons C_{(g)} + 2D_{(g)}$, what will happen if you increase the pressure?

3. Given the reaction $4A_{(s)} + B_{(g)} \rightleftharpoons 2C_{(s)} + 3D_{(s)}$, if you increase the concentration of A what will happen to the reaction?

4. What is the difference between an exothermic reaction and an endothermic reaction?

5. How is the equilibrium affected if you add heat to an exothermic reaction?

6. How is equilibrium affected if you increase the pressure in the following reaction?

$2SO_{3(g)} \rightleftharpoons 2SO_{2(g)} + O_{2(g)}$

ANSWERS

CHECK YOUR ANSWERS

1. Le Châtelier's Principle states that when an external stress is applied to a system in chemical equilibrium, the equilibrium will change to reduce the effects of the stress.

2. Here, nothing will happen if you increase the pressure. The number of moles of reactant are equal to the number of moles of product.

3. The reaction will shift RIGHT to make more products.

4. In an endothermic reaction, energy is used (absorbed) by the reactants to create the products. In an exothermic reaction, energy is given off (released) during the creation of the products.

5. Adding heat to an exothermic reaction will cause the reaction to shift LEFT because heat is a product of the reaction.

6. Three molecules of gas are on the right-hand side, and two molecules of gas are on the left. The reaction will shift LEFT so that the pressure is reduced and the stress on the system is minimized.

Unit 12

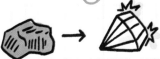

Thermodynamics

Chapter 34

THE FIRST LAW OF THERMODYNAMICS

ENERGY

Every chemical reaction obeys both the LAW OF CONSERVATION OF MASS and the LAW OF CONSERVATION OF ENERGY.

The law of conservation of energy states that the total energy of an isolated system is constant.

This means that within an isolated system, energy can be changed or transformed, but it cannot be created or destroyed. This is also known as the **FIRST LAW OF THERMODYNAMICS**.

> **THE FIRST LAW OF THERMODYNAMICS**
> Energy can be converted from one form to
> another but cannot be created or destroyed.

ENERGY is the capacity to do work. In chemistry, work is defined as change in energy, resulting from a process.

Types of Energy

RADIANT ENERGY is the energy of electromagnetic waves. For example, we receive energy from the sun via radiation.

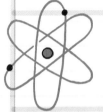

THERMAL ENERGY Energy associated with the random motion of atoms and molecules.

CHEMICAL ENERGY Energy stored within the bonds of chemical compounds/substances.

POTENTIAL ENERGY (PE) Energy that is available because of the object's position; also called **stored energy**.

KINETIC ENERGY (KE) Energy that is produced by a moving object; also called the **energy of motion**.

Almost every chemical reaction absorbs or releases energy, usually in the form of heat.

Heat is the transfer of thermal energy between two substances at different temperatures.

- Heat can flow: It moves from a substance that is hot to a substance that is cold.

- Heat can be absorbed: The substance takes in heat.

- Heat can be released, or given off, during an energy change.

THERMOCHEMISTRY is the study of the heat change in a chemical reaction. Thermochemistry is a part of a bigger subject, called **THERMODYNAMICS**. Thermodynamics is the study of the relationships between heat and other forms of energy within a system.

CALORIMETRY, SPECIFIC HEAT, AND HEAT CAPACITY

To measure heat changes in both physical and chemical reactions, scientists use **CALORIMETRY**. Calorimetry is the process of measuring the amount of heat released or absorbed during a chemical reaction. A special container in a closed system called a **CALORIMETER** is used. This method determines, through scientific experiment, if a reaction is exothermic or endothermic.

The main type of calorimeter is a COFFEE-CUP CALORIMETER, which stays at constant pressure.

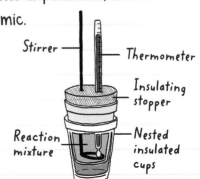

Stirrer — Thermometer

Insulating stopper

Reaction mixture — Nested insulated cups

455

To calculate the heat change, you need to know the specific heat of the substance.

SPECIFIC HEAT (C) is the amount of heat required to raise the temperature of 1 g of the substance by 1°C (units are joules/grams/°C). Specific-heat capacity can be reported in the units of calories per gram degree Celsius, too.

Use this equation to find the amount of heat that has been absorbed or released (heat energy, Joules):

1 calorie = 4.184 J

$$q = mc\Delta t$$

Δt is a change in temperature in Kelvin (K) or Celsius (C):

final temperature − initial temperature = $t_{final} - t_{initial}$

m is the mass of a substance (kg)
c is the specific heat (J/kgK)

HEATING AND COOLING CURVES

Another way of showing what happens during a phase change is to use a heating or cooling curve. This graph shows a heating curve that illustrates the temperature of the substance vs the amount of heat absorbed, and its phase changes.

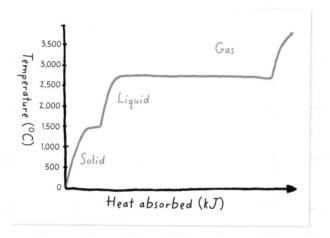

- As substances heat up, they absorb energy and change state. A **solid state** is shown on the lower left-hand end of the graph. That means it has low temperature and very little absorbed heat.

- As the heat is increased, the line rises until enough energy is absorbed that the substance turns into a liquid. The same occurs when the state changes from liquid to gas.

The line stays flat during the change of state because the substance needs to absorb enough heat to weaken the forces of attraction.

This graph shows the phase changes of 1 kg of water as it passes from ice at –50°C to steam at temperatures above 100°C.

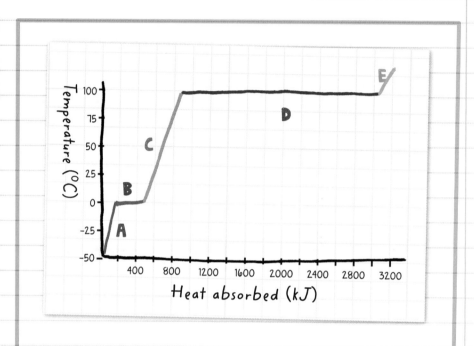

Reading the curve:

A   Rise in temperature as solid ice absorbs heat.
B   Absorption of heat of fusion to melt the solid.
C   Rise in temperature as liquid water absorbs heat.
D   Water boils and absorbs heat of vaporization.
E   Steam absorbs heat and increases its temperature.

1. Find q_{water}.

The calorimeter is an isolated system, so

> Use density = 1g/ml to convert 125 ml to 125 g

> heat released by the copper ball

$q_{cu} + q_{water} = 0$ OR $-q_{cu} = q_{water}$

> heat absorbed by water

$q_{water} = mc\Delta t = (125\ g)\ (4.184\ J/g/°C)\ (28.6°C - 25.0°C) = 1882.8\ J$

2. Solve for specific heat of Cu.

The heat absorbed by the water is equal to the heat lost by the copper. That makes the copper exothermic.

$q_{cu} = -mc\Delta t = (32.5)\ c\ (28.6 - 122) = -490$

$Cu = .318\ J/g/°C$

The heat of the copper ball = -1882.8 J/g/°C

ENTHALPY

Scientists have developed a way to determine how much heat energy is in a system, called **ENTHALPY**. Enthalpy is represented by H.

Enthalpy is equal to the internal energy of the system plus its pressure and volume.

$$H = E + PV$$

The change in enthalpy (ΔH) tells you how much enthalpy (heat) was gained or lost in a system.

$$\Delta H = \Delta E + (\Delta) PV$$

OR if the pressure is constant, use this equation:

$$\Delta H = \Delta E + P\Delta V$$

Since the pressure is constant no change symbol, Δ.

Enthalpy of Reactions

$(\Delta H) = \Sigma H \text{ (products)} - \Sigma H \text{ (reactants)}$

means "the sum of"

for a normal chemical reaction that goes from reactants → products.

$\Delta H > 0$: endothermic process (energy is absorbed by the system)

$\Delta H < 0$: exothermic process (energy is released from the system)

$\Delta H = 0$: no change to the system

Another way to think of enthalpy:

If you have $100 in your wallet and you buy two movie tickets for a total of $40, how much do you have left? $60. The problem, written as an enthalpy equation, would look like this: $H = 60 - 100 = -40$. The answer is negative because you used up $40.

FOR EXAMPLE: Calculate the heat evolved when 13.56 g of oxygen (O_2) is used to burn white phosphorous at standard temperature and pressure according to the equation.

$$P_{4(s)} + 5O_{2(g)} \rightarrow P_4O_{10(s)} \qquad \Delta H = -3013 \text{ kJ/mol}$$

1. Balance the equation.

$$P_{4(s)} + 5O_{2(g)} \rightarrow P_4O_{10(s)}$$

2. Find the enthalpy ratio.

$$\frac{-3013 \text{ kJ/mol}}{5 \text{ mol } O_2}$$

3. Solve for heat evolved. $\leftarrow$ $\boxed{1 \text{ mol } O_2 = 32.00}$

$$\Delta H = 13.56 \text{ g } O_2 \times \frac{1 \text{ mol } O_2}{31.998 \text{ g } O_2} \times \frac{-3013 \text{ kJ/mol}}{5 \text{ mol } O_2}$$

= −255.4 kJ of heat given off when oxygen is
used to burn white phosphorous.

Why is enthalpy useful?

When writing a thermochemical equation, you can tell if
the reaction will be exothermic (absorb heat) or endothermic
(release heat).

In this equation, methane (CH_4) undergoes combustion, and
the reaction looks like this:

$$CH_{4(g)} + 2O_{2(g)} \rightarrow 2H_2O_{(l)} + CO_{2(g)} \quad \Delta H = -802.94 \text{ kJ/mol}$$

You can come up with the following relationships:

1 mol of CH_4 = 2 mol O_2 = 1 mol CO_2 = 2 mol H_2O = ΔH
= −802.94 kJ/mol

Rules for writing thermochemical equations:

1. Always specify the physical state of the substance. This is important because different states can have different enthalpies. For example, the enthalpy of liquid water to water vapor changes by 44.0 kJ/mol.

2. If you multiply both sides of the equation by a number, n, you must also multiply the enthalpy by the same number.

For example, if you now have 2 mol liquid water converted to 2 mol water vapor, the enthalpy is 88.0 kJ/mol.

3. When the equation is reversed, the sign of H reverses. No recalculation is needed because the products and reactants have changed places. This can affect the enthalpy.

For example: If the reaction above is reversed, instead of releasing 802.94 kJ/mol, the reaction produces it.

When you are working with equations, you need to know the STANDARD ENTHALPY OF FORMATION ($\Delta H°_f$) for each substance.

The standard enthalpy of formation is equal to the change in enthalpy when 1 mol of a substance in the standard state (1 atm pressure and 298.15° K) is formed from its pure elements under the same conditions. The standard temperature is different in thermodynamic calculations, because it is not the STP that is used for gases.

> The enthalpy of a reaction is calculated using the formula:
> $$H_{rxn} = (H \text{ products}) - (H \text{ reactants})$$

Calculate the enthalpy of reaction for the following equation (use a table of standard enthalpies to get the enthalpies for each substance):

$$C_2H_{4(g)} + 3O_{2(g)} \rightarrow 2CO_{2(g)} + 2H_2O_{(g)}$$

1. Find the enthalpies of formation of the products.

$\Delta H°_f$ of CO_2 = -393.5 kJ/mol

$\Delta H°_f$ of H_2O = -241.8 kJ/mol

That is the ΔH of formation ($\Delta H°_f$) for 1 mol of each substance. You will need to multiply that number to equal the number of moles in the equation.

$\Delta H°_f$ of CO_2 = –393.5 kJ/mol × 2 = –787.0 kJ/mol

$\Delta H°_f$ of H_2O = –241.8 kJ/mol × 2 = –483.6 kJ/mol

2. Find the enthalpies of formation of the reactants.

$\Delta H°_f$ of O_2 = 0.00 kJ/mol (The enthalphy of a naturally occurring element is always = 0.)

$\Delta H°_f$ of C_2H_4 = –61.05 kJ/mol × 1 = –61.05

3. Calculate the enthalpy of the reaction by using the following equation:

$\Delta H°$ = $\Delta H°_f$ (products) – $\Delta H°_f$ (reactants)
[(–787.0 + (–483.6)] – [–61.05] = –1209.55 kJ

The reaction is exothermic because the change in enthalpy is negative, indicating that energy is released.

FOR EXAMPLE: Calculate $\Delta H°$ for the combustion of methane.

1. Write the balanced equation.

$$CH_{4(g)} + 2\ O_{2(g)} \rightarrow CO_{2(g)} + 2\ H_2O_{(g)}$$

2. Write the enthalpies for each substance.

$\Delta H°_f$ of CO_2 = -393.5 kJ/mol × 1 = -393.5 kJ/mol

$\Delta H°_f$ of H_2O = -241.8 kJ/mol × 2 = -483.6 kJ/mol

$\Delta H°_f$ of CH_4 = -74.5 kJ/mol × 1 = -74.5 kJ/mol

$\Delta H°_f$ of O_2 = 0, because it is elemental

3. Write the equation to solve for ΔH.

= [-393.5 kJ + 2 × (-241.8 kJ)] - [-74.5 kJ + 2 × (0 kJ)]

= -802.6 kJ

HESS'S LAW

Swiss chemist GERMAIN HESS found a solution for scientists who couldn't directly perform a chemical reaction to determine the standard enthalpy of formation ($\Delta H°_f$) of a substance.

He devised HESS'S LAW, which calculates a reaction's enthalpy change even when it cannot be measured directly. It's like taking an indirect route because you can't go straight.

> Hess's Law states that when reactants are converted into products, the change in enthalpy is the same regardless of how many steps it takes to get to the end product.

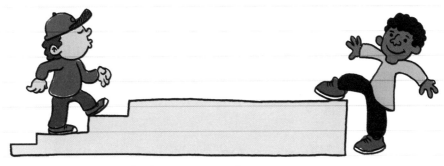

Hess's Law: Whether you go up four steps or just one, you will still expend the same total amount of energy.

FOR EXAMPLE: Calculate the enthalpy for the following reaction:

$N_{2(g)} + 2O_{2(g)} \rightarrow 2NO_{2(g)}$, given that

$N_{2(g)} + O_{2(g)} \rightarrow 2NO_{(g)} = +180$ kJ,

$2NO_{2(g)} \rightarrow 2NO_{(g)} + O_{2(g)}$ and $\Delta H° = +112$ kJ

1. Reverse the second equation so that it will fit with the original equation.

$$N_{2(g)} + O_{2(g)} \rightarrow 2NO_{(g)} \qquad \Delta H° = +180 \text{ kJ}$$

$$2NO_{(g)} + O_{2(g)} \rightarrow 2NO_{2(g)} \qquad \Delta H° = -112 \text{ kJ}$$

When you reverse the equation, you MUST reverse the sign, so +112 kJ becomes –112 kJ.

2. Add the two equations together and eliminate identical items. This means that you are also adding the two enthalpies together.

$$N_{2(g)} + 2O_{2(g)} \rightarrow 2NO_{2(g)} \qquad \Delta H° = [+180] + [-112] = +68 \text{ kJ}$$

CHECK YOUR KNOWLEDGE

1. Define the Law of Conservation of Energy and the First Law of Thermodynamics. How are they related?

2. Name and describe three of the five types of energy.

3. What is the difference between heat and thermal energy?

4. If a reaction is endothermic, is energy absorbed or released?

5. What is enthalpy and what does a change in enthalpy tell you about the system?

6. Explain what happens when the change in enthalpy (ΔH) is > 0, < 0, and = 0.

7. What is the standard enthalpy of formation ($\Delta H°_f$)?

8. What happens if you can't perform a chemical reaction to determine the standard enthalpy of formation ($\Delta H°_f$) of a substance? Which law do you use? Define the law.

ANSWERS 469

1. The Law of Conservation of Energy states that the total energy of an isolated system is constant. The First Law of Thermodynamics states that energy can be converted from one form to another but cannot be created or destroyed. They both say basically the same thing, that within an isolated system, energy can be changed or transformed, but it cannot be created or destroyed.

2. Radiant energy is the energy of electromagnetic waves, thermal energy is energy that is associated with the random motion of atoms and molecules, chemical energy is energy that is stored within the bonds of chemical compounds/substances, potential energy is energy that is available because of the object's position, and kinetic energy is the energy that is produced by a moving object.

3. Thermal energy depends on the kinetic energy of the substance. Heat is the transfer of energy from one substance to another.

4. An endothermic system is one in which heat is absorbed by the reactants (ΔH is +).

5. A change in enthalpy (ΔH) tells you how much enthalpy (heat) was gained or lost in a system.

6. $\Delta H > 0$ is an endothermic process (energy is absorbed by the system), $\Delta H < 0$ is an exothermic process (energy is released from the system), and $\Delta H = 0$ is no change to the system.

7. The standard enthalpy of formation ($\Delta H°_f$) is equal to the change in enthalpy when 1 mol of a substance in the standard state (1 atm pressure and 298.15° K) is formed from its pure elements under the same conditions. The standard enthalpy of formation values for pure elements is zero.

8. If you can't perform a chemical reaction to determine the standard enthalpy of formation, use Hess's Law. This states that when reactants are converted into products, the TOTAL change in enthalpy for the overall reaction is the SUM of the changes in enthalpy of the multiple stages or steps that are necessary to reach the end product.

Chapter 35

THE SECOND LAW OF THERMODYNAMICS

ENTROPY

To predict the spontaneity of a reaction (how, why, and when a reaction will occur), scientists use a thermodynamic function called **ENTROPY (S)**. Entropy is measured in Joules per kelvin.

ENTROPY (S)
A measure of disorder (uncertainty or randomness) within a system; a principle of thermodynamics that refers to the idea that the universe tends to move toward a disordered state.

   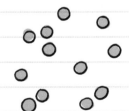

order ⟶ disorder

SECOND LAW OF THERMODYNAMICS

The easiest way to determine whether a reaction will be spontaneous is to look at its change in entropy. The **SECOND LAW OF THERMODYNAMICS** explains this relationship.

> **SECOND LAW OF THERMODYNAMICS**
> The state of entropy in an isolated system over the entire universe will always increase.

This means every process will want to move from order to disorder. Therefore, disorder is much more probable than order. This also applies to chemical reactions.

During a reaction, the change in entropy is measured as ΔS_{system}, where $\Delta S_{sys} > 0$ and the system becomes more disordered during the reaction.

A positive ΔS value is nature's preference, compared to a negative ΔH value (exothermic).

In $\Delta S_{sys} < 0$, the system becomes less disordered during the reaction.

Things to know!

- Solids have the most order. Liquids are more disordered than solids, and gases are more disordered than liquids. So, in order of entropy:

  solids < liquids < gas

- Any process/reaction that increases the number of particles in the system increases the amount of disorder.

  more particles → greater disorder

The change in entropy of a reaction is equal to the sum of the standard entropy of the products minus the sum of the standard entropy of the reactants.

ΔS_{rxn} means a change in entropy.

$S_{rxn} = \Sigma$ standard entropy of the products $- \Sigma$ standard entropy of the reactants

---

FOR EXAMPLE: Calculate the standard entropy change of the following reaction:

$2CO_{(g)} + O_{2(g)} \rightarrow 2CO_{2(g)}$

1. Write the equation for ΔS_{rxn}.

standard molar entropy, measured in J/mol K (Joules per mole Kelvin)

$\Delta S_{rxn} = [S° \, CO_2 \times 2 \text{ mol}] - [(S° \, CO)(2 \text{ mol}) + S° \, O_2]$

products - reactants

2. Fill in the S° given that

$S° \, CO_2 = 213.64$ J/mol K $S° \, CO = 197.91$ J/mol K
$S° \, O = 205.3$ J/mol K

$S_{rxn} = [213.64 \text{ J/mol K} \times 2 \text{ mol}] - [(197.91 \text{ J/mol K})(2 \text{ mol}) + 205.3 \text{ J/mol K}] = -173.84$ J/K

"mol" gets canceled, the S_{rxn} is expressed in Joules/Kelvin.

The entropy indicates that the reaction becomes less disordered. This is correct because there are fewer molecules in the products than in the reactants.

SPONTANEOUS OR NOT?

Some reactions have spontaneity because they become more disordered (ΔS), but others are spontaneous because they give off energy in the form of heat (they are exothermic).

The GIBBS FREE ENERGY (G) function relates the entropy and enthalpy of a reaction.

> **GIBBS FREE ENERGY**
> The energy from a chemical reaction used to do work.

SPONTANEOUS means "yes, the reaction will happen."

NONSPONTANEOUS means "no, the reaction will not happen."

Spontaneous, in this context, has nothing to do with the rate or speed (how fast/slow) at which a reaction will happen. Sometimes, the phrase THERMODYNAMICALLY FAVORABLE is used, which means that in terms of heat and disorder, the reaction occurs.

> $\Delta G = \Delta H - T \Delta S$
> for all reactions.

ΔG tells you whether or not it will happen.

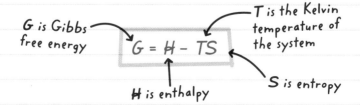

G is Gibbs free energy

$G = H - TS$

T is the Kelvin temperature of the system

S is entropy

H is enthalpy

If you want to know the standard-state conditions (where $T = 298K$), the reaction becomes

$$\Delta G° = \Delta H° - \Delta TS°$$

Things to know!

- $\Delta G° < 0$ is spontaneous.

- $\Delta G° > 0$ is not spontaneous.

- $\Delta G° = 0$ means that the reaction is at equilibrium.

Systems in nature tend to have exothermic heat ($-\Delta H$), and tend toward more disorder ($+\Delta S$), so they have a negative Gibbs value.

CHECK YOUR KNOWLEDGE

1. To predict the spontaneity of a reaction, scientists use a thermodynamic function called _____.

2. Order the physical phases of a substance from least disordered to most ordered.

3. Does the universe tend to move more toward an orderly system or a disordered system? Which of these has greater entropy?

4. What is the sign of the entropy change for the following reactions?

   A. $U_{(s)} + 3F_{2(g)} \rightarrow UF_{6(g)}$
   B. $PCl_{3(l)} + Cl_{2(g)} \rightarrow PCl_{5(s)}$

5. What is the Gibbs free energy function and why is it important?

6. If $G° < 0$, is the reaction favorable? What does this mean?

ANSWERS

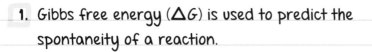

CHECK YOUR ANSWERS

1. Gibbs free energy (ΔG) is used to predict the spontaneity of a reaction.

2. From least to most disorderd: solid, liquid, and gas.

3. The universe tends to move more toward a disordered system, which has more entropy ($\Delta S > 0$).

4. A. $\Delta S < 0$ because the number of gas particles decreases.

   B. $\Delta S < 0$ because the number of total particles decreases.

5. The Gibbs free energy (G) function relates entropy and enthalpy of a reaction. $\Delta G = \Delta H - \Delta TS$, where H is enthalpy, G is Gibbs free energy, T is Kelvin temperature of the system, and S is entropy, is important because it determines whether a reaction is spontaneous.

6. $\Delta G° < 0$ is a favorable reaction, meaning that the reaction is spontaneous (it will happen).

Chapter 36

REACTION RATES

Scientists want to know how fast (or slow) a reaction will proceed. To get that information, they determine its **REACTION RATE**, the change in concentration of the reactant or product over time. Reaction rate is measured in molarity/second (M/s).

> **Thermodynamics** tells you the *direction* in which a reaction is going (will it happen or not?) but does not tell you anything about the speed. **Kinetics** is the branch of chemistry that deals with *speed* or *rate of chemical reactions*.

THERMODYNAMICS

KINETICS

Common reaction rates and their speeds:

Photosynthesis (how plants convert sunlight to energy) is relatively fast.

Coal turns to diamond under great pressure and very slowly (about one billion years).

Wet cement drying happens slowly (it can take 28 days to fully cure).

WET CEMENT

Reaction rates are important because they give scientists an idea of how long the reaction will take to complete.

In the equation,

$A \rightarrow B$, A is the reactant, and B is the product.

As the reaction proceeds, the concentration of the reactants (A) will decrease, and the concentration of the product (B) will increase.

The AVERAGE REACTION RATE is determined by calculating the change in concentration over time.

The formula for the average reaction rate for $A \rightarrow B$ is

$$\text{Rate} = \frac{-\Delta[A]}{\Delta t} \quad \text{OR} \quad \text{Rate} = \frac{\Delta[B]}{\Delta t}$$

where Δt is the change in time. (The change in the reactants is a negative, because the reactants are being consumed.)

$[A]$ and $[B]$ are given in molarity (mol/L), and t can be measured in seconds, minutes, days, or the unit of time that is most appropriate for the time scale of the reaction.

Reaction rates can be graphed. A reaction rate graph will look like this:

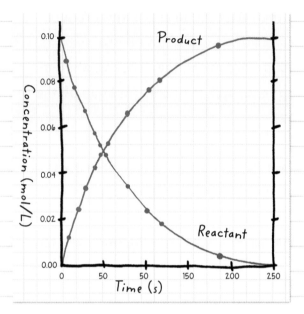

At the start of a chemical reaction, the product concentration (blue line) is zero. As time progresses, the concentration of the reactants (red line) decreases and the concentration of the product increases. The point at which the rates of the forward and reverse reactions are the same is the chemical equilibrium.

COLLISION THEORY

For a chemical reaction to happen, the atoms must interact. This usually means that they collide with each other. The greater the concentration (the more molecules that you have) the more collisions that you will have.

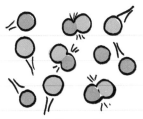 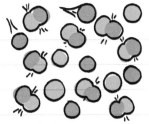

Low concentration = fewer collisions   High concentration = more collisions

Not all collisons will produce a new substance. Collisions require the right orientation and proper energy to produce a new substance.

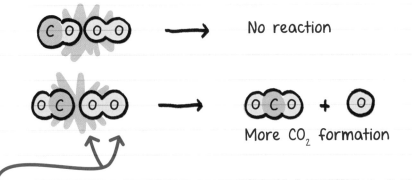

C O O O $\longrightarrow$ No reaction

O C O O $\longrightarrow$ O C O + O

More CO_2 formation

When CO reacts with O_2 gas, the C atom must be involved in the collision for a new product, CO_2, to be formed.

The way in which the collisions occur also plays a role in the speed of reaction. If the atoms collide with minimum energy and a favorable orientation, the atoms will have an EFFECTIVE COLLISION, and this will result in a reaction. Factors such as increased temperature and surface area increase the number of effective collisions in a chemical reaction.

Different ways that collisions can occur between molecules:

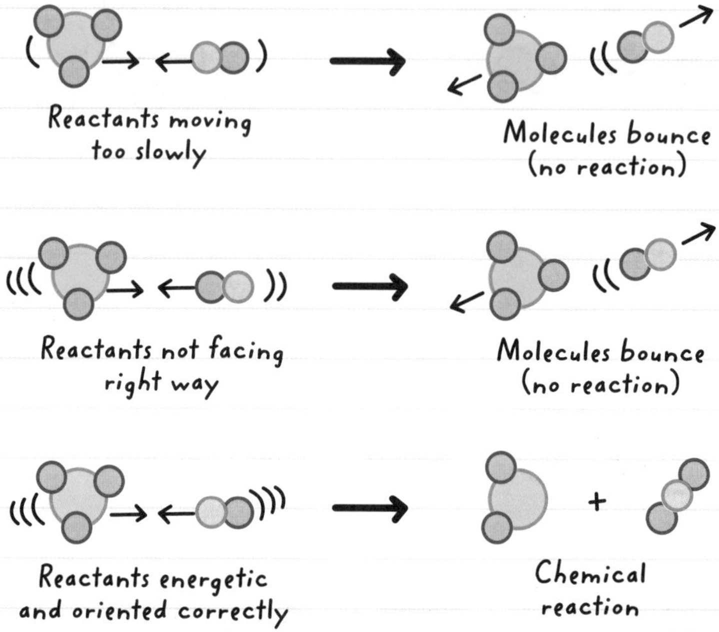

Reactants moving
too slowly

Molecules bounce
(no reaction)

Reactants not facing
right way

Molecules bounce
(no reaction)

Reactants energetic
and oriented correctly

Chemical
reaction

FACTORS THAT AFFECT REACTION RATES

Reaction rate can be increased or decreased based on the following factors:

TEMPERATURE **Increasing temperature** increases the kinetic energy (movement of the particles), and they will collide more, increasing the reaction rate.

Decreasing temperature usually slows down reaction rate.

CONCENTRATION Increasing the concentration of the reactants increases the reaction rate, because there are more particles to react and collide.

Decreasing the concentration reduces the reaction rate.

SURFACE AREA Increasing surface area of the reactant by crushing it or cutting it allows for more spaces on the substance to interact and collide. This increases the reaction rate.

Decreasing surface area decreases the reaction rate.

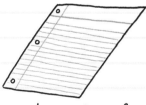

This paper has greater surface area because there is more of it that can interact with another object.

This wad of paper has less surface area exposed, so it does not have as many opportunities to react with another substance.

A boulder has less *surface area* than an equal mass of pebbles! Surface area is the outside layer/exterior of a substance. More of the total area of the pebble is exposed to the outside than the boulder, which has most of its area beneath the surface.

CATALYST A catalyst is a substance that is used to increase the reaction rate, but it is not consumed during the reaction. A catalyst increases reaction rate by decreasing the ACTIVATION ENERGY.

An example of a catalyst is an enzyme. Enzymes are proteins that act as catalysts in biochemical reactions. The OXIDATION of glucose, the biological process by which organisms obtain energy, depends on enzymes to make the process go faster.

Activation Energy

The **ACTIVATION ENERGY (E_a)** is the minimum amount of energy needed to start a chemical reaction.

Every molecule has its own minimum amount of kinetic energy. If two molecules interact, their collision must have enough energy to overcome the activation

> The lower the activation energy, the faster a reaction will proceed. The higher the activation energy, the more slowly a reaction will proceed.

energy needed for the reaction. The reaction must also possess enough free energy (ΔG) to break the bonds between the molecules so that they can react. Therefore, activation energy is related to free energy.

ΔG = Gibbs free energy, or the difference in energy between products and reactants.

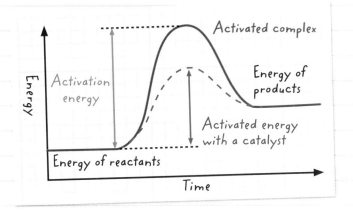

The graph shows that reactants must overcome the activation energy before they can combine (into the activated complex) and become products.

Without a catalyst, the activation energy is higher, shown by the blue curve.

With a catalyst, the activation energy is lower, shown by the red curve.

The reaction must have enough energy in its collisions to break the bonds within the molecules and react to form the product.

Activation energy is also related to the activation enthalpy ΔH:

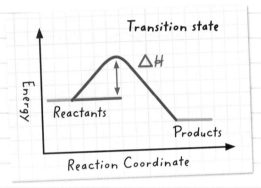

Activation enthalpy represents the difference in energy between the reactants at their normal state (shown by the purple line at the beginning of the curve) and their transition state at the top of the curve (leads to the activation energy) in a reaction.

As E_a and ΔH decrease, the reaction has a greater chance of occurring. As E_a and ΔH increase, the reaction has less of a chance of occurring.

REACTION MECHANISMS AND THE RATE-DETERMINING STEP

Chemical reactions occur based on a specific **REACTION MECHANISM**, a series of steps that allows the reactants to undergo several reactions to form the desired product. Each part of the mechanism shows the point at which bonds are broken within the molecules, and new bonds are formed. Each mechanism proceeds at its own rate of reaction, which determines the overall rate of reaction of the process.

Two things to know:

1. The overall rate of reaction must be equal to the sum of each mechanism's rate of reaction.

2. The **RATE-DETERMINING** step of the reaction will determine the reaction rate of the overall reaction.

> **RATE-DETERMINING STEP**
> The slowest mechanism (reaction)
> within the overall chemical reaction.

FOR EXAMPLE: In the reaction $NO_2 + CO \rightarrow NO + CO_2$:

Nitrogen dioxide combines with carbon monoxide to yield nitrogen oxide and carbon dioxide. This is not a one-step reaction. Instead, it takes place in two smaller reactions. Each reaction has its own rate.

The first reaction is $NO_2 + NO_2 \rightarrow NO + NO_3$. (This happens at a slow rate.)

The second reaction is $NO_3 + CO \rightarrow NO_2 + CO_2$. (This happens at a fast rate.)

We don't write the entire reaction as two steps, because molecules that are on the left and right of the reaction cancel out:

$NO_2 + NO_2 \rightarrow NO + NO_3$ (slow)

$NO_3 + CO \rightarrow NO_2 + CO_2$ (fast)

Final equation: $NO_2 + CO \rightarrow NO + CO_2$

The rate-determining step was the first reaction because it is the slowest.

CHECK YOUR KNOWLEDGE

1. What is the reaction rate and what are its units?

2. What three conditions can speed up or slow down the reaction rate?

3. Define surface area. Give an example of it.

4. What is activation energy and what part does it play in a chemical reaction?

5. How does the rate-determining step affect the overall reaction rate?

ANSWERS 493

1. The reaction rate is the change in concentration of the reactant or product over time. It is measured in molarity/second.

2. Change in temperature, concentration, or surface area can speed up or slow down reaction rate.

3. Surface area is the outside layer/exterior of a substance. Sugar has more surface area when bought in a bag at the store than if condensed into a hard candy.

4. Activation energy is the minimum amount of energy needed to start a chemical reaction. The level of activation energy affects the speed at which a reaction will proceed.

5. The overall reaction rate depends almost entirely on the rate of the slowest step.

☆ INDEX ☆

495